Controlling Corporate Illegality

The Regulatory Justice System

Nancy Frank
Michael Lombness

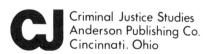

Criminal Justice Studies
Anderson Publishing Co.
Cincinnati, Ohio

To Bill

To Anita and Paul

CONTENTS

CHAPTER 1

Corporate Illegality
and Regulatory Justice

The nightly news is filled with stories of death and predation, cheating and lying, fraud and folly. In an earlier era, the villain in each of these stories was an individual, sometimes a gang, occasionally a mob. They fit a demographic profile that placed them at the bottom of the social hierarchy. We had little problem deciding what to do about them and their miserable acts—they should be punished and (sometimes) rehabilitated if possible.

Times have changed. Today, the nightly news brings us these same evil stories, but the culprits have changed. Today, the culprit is likely to be a corporation. Corporate crime has increased dramatically, probably due largely to the fact that more and more of the things we do today are done by or within corporations. "As a consequence, when something goes wrong, whether a toxic spill or a swindle, chances are good that a corporation will be implicated" (Stone, 1985: 13). Not only are corporations implicated in more and more of the nasty acts we perpetrate against one another, but good-old-fashioned "lock 'em up" solutions do not appear to work very well when applied to corporate illegality (Stone, 1975: 50-56).

These changes have been developing over the course of the past 100 years. Since the Industrial Revolution of the nineteenth century, sweeping technological and economic changes have offered greater health, comfort, and enjoyment. Unfortunately, this progress, while improving the quality of life, has had costs as well. For each modern improvement, some accompanying problem can usually be identified. Mountains of trash and oceans of hazardous waste are a testament to the convenience of throw-away products and the wonders of plastics and synthetics. An epidemic of cancer and birth defects appears to be the tragic consequence of food additives, drugs, and a chemical environment with unknown side-effects. By the end of the nineteenth century, numerous laws already had been passed to deal with a wide range of troubles caused by corporations. But perhaps the biggest change has been described as a revolution in government (MacDonagh, 1958)—the creation of the regulatory justice system.

Regulation has grown in spurts, with most major regulatory agencies having their origins in one of three distinct, and relatively short, periods (Vogel, 1981). During the Progressive Era at the turn of the century, re-

1

formers became concerned about the total lack of control over the exploitative nature of some segments of American business. Responding to the tug of emotion aroused by factory fires, coal mine disasters, and railroad casualties, legislators responded by creating specialized agencies to control corporations. For example, Upton Sinclair's 1905 best-seller, *The Jungle*, which described filthy conditions in slaughterhouses and putrid meat products being sold, brought conditions in the meat-packing industry to the attention of the public and Congress and was a major factor in the passage of the Meat Inspection Act and the Food and Drug Act of 1906, which regulated the sanitary conditions of meat and food processing. During this same period, farmers and small businessmen became concerned about the growing economic power of "the trusts" and the "great combines," large corporations in basic industries which seemed to threaten the equilibrium of the economic system. Antitrust legislation and regulations aimed at preventing monopolies were created to control the economic power of large corporations. Rather than relying on tort actions or general criminal statutes, which often proved impotent to control corporate irresponsibility, these agencies were given the authority to write specialized rules and to enforce the rules with special powers.

During the Great Depression of the 1930s, a new wave of regulatory action focused on economic institutions. The depression was widely perceived as having been caused by reckless banking practices and speculative stock transactions. As a result, banks and securities investments came under strict regulatory control with the creation of the Federal Deposit Insurance Corporation (FDIC) and the Securities and Exchange Commission (SEC). In addition to providing control, these agencies also provided services by stabilizing and legitimizing financial institutions which had lost the public's trust and confidence.

The most recent spurt in regulatory activity occurred during the Great Society Era of 1960s and early 1970s. During this time, industry practices affecting health, safety and the environment became the "problems" which reformers sought to correct through regulatory controls. Federal regulatory agencies were created to protect worker health and safety, the environment, and consumer product safety.

This most recent wave of regulation has resulted in the most dramatic changes and has brought with it a flurry of criticism that regulation has become an invasive and all-pervasive force that has gotten seriously out of hand. Almost a century after the creation of the regulatory justice system, this governmental invention has grown to enormous proportions. Corporations spend literally billions of dollars annually complying with regulations, and still we constantly hear of scandals and tragedies, with a corporation at the center of the plot. If regulatory agencies were designed to control corporate behavior, they do not seem to be doing very well.

One does not have to look far to find criticisms and outright condemnation of the regulatory system. A remarkable aspect of all this criticism, however, is a surprising lack of agreement about what is wrong with regulation. Regulatory agencies have been criticized for a variety of other defects, leading to the conclusion that regulation is at best ineffective, and at worst a costly drag on the economy (see, for example, Mendeloff, 1979). Legal scholars have suggested that the law may be inherently flawed as a means of controlling corporate conduct and instilling corporate responsibility (Stone, 1975). Political scientists have noted that the politics of regulation frequently lead to distortions of regulatory policy (Wilson, 1980). Economists studying regulation have totted up the costs and benefits of regulation and have questioned whether the benefits are worth the enormous costs. And business managers complain of increased paperwork and interference from government regulators.

To some, regulatory agencies have tried to do too much, building a labyrinth of rules but producing few constructive results. To others, the problem is that there are too few rules, that the serious problems requiring regulation have not yet been addressed, and that regulatory agencies are too timid in their regulatory efforts. On the one hand, regulators are caricatured as bumbling and stumbling along with enormous feet, squashing creative and productive efforts as it thumps across the economic landscape. On the other, regulation is seen as a pesky fly, occasionally annoying but having little effect as it rides on the back of the great horse of American industry.

Our own view lies somewhere between these two extremes. The validity of all of these complaints depends upon which agencies one is looking at and at what time in history. Over the course of the past ten years, the pendulum of regulatory policy has swung dramatically. With these wide and dramatic policy shifts, errors of excess may have been committed on all sides. During the muscle-stretching period of the 1970s, regulators perhaps became too enamored of their power, and neglected consensus-building efforts that would be crucial to the long-term stability and legitimacy of regulatory agencies. Many of these agencies subsequently had their wings clipped during the deregulatory backlash of the 1980s. Here, too, excessive zeal caused reformers to approach their work with a meat ax when they should have been using a scalpel.

Meanwhile, thousands of state and local regulatory agencies were muddling along as usual, largely insulated from national moods and federal policies. Situated in a stable environment, free of reformers on either side of the great regulatory controversies brewing in Washington, state and local agencies simply carried on much as federal agencies had up to the mid-1960s.

With such dramatic goings-on in Washington, scholars and social critics have focused their sites on federal regulation. Much has been learned from the studies and analyses of successive reforms of federal regulatory policy. Nonetheless, the forces that shook the federal agencies simply did not materialize at the state and local levels. Thus, although we are aware of the controversies surrounding federal regulation, our own evaluation of "the problem with regulation" focuses on those problems that beset the large majority of regulatory agencies.

Given this focus, our work is founded on two principal assumptions. First, regulation and regulatory agencies are here to stay, even at the federal level. Despite recent deregulatory efforts aimed at curbing regulatory initiatives, regulation will remain one of the most important governmental institutions for controlling corporations (Weidenbaum, 1977). Second, regulatory action could be greatly improved. We have learned a great deal from the reform efforts of the 1970s and the deregulatory reactions of the 1980s. Despite their excesses, each has illuminated the dilemmas of reform and the unintended side effects of alternative regulatory policies.

This book is intended as a primer in the structure and processes of the regulatory justice system. It reviews some of the important legal features of the regulatory justice system, as well as the social forces that press on the regulatory system to form regulatory action. It focuses on regulation as one of the primary systems available for controlling corporate illegality.

Corporate Illegality and Regulatory Justice

In 1949, Edwin Sutherland published his seminal work on "white-collar crime," coining the phrase and creating a new area of specialization for criminologists. Through the 1950s and 1960s, scholars sporadically published research on white-collar crime, usually dealing with the offenses of individuals or with economic crimes, such as anti-trust offenses (see, for example, Cressey, 1953; Geis, 1967). During the late 1970s, however, the focus of attention shifted toward the illegal acts of corporations, particularly those offenses that cause physical harm to consumers, workers, and the environment (see, for example, Clinard and Yeager, 1980; Ermann and Lundman, 1978; Geis and Stotland, 1980; Reiman, 1979). Not coincidentally, this academic interest in the problem of corporate deviance corresponded to an increase in the amount of law relating to risky and harmful corporate behavior.

Initially, criminologists limited their examination of "corporate crime" to criminal offenses by corporations and tended to focus on questions of causation—in other words, why corporations commit crime. With this focus came an interest in deterrence and studies of the sanctions meted out to corporations. Scholars soon discovered what Sutherland had noted thirty years earlier: the study of "white-collar" or "corporate" crime requires an examination of illegal acts outside the boundaries of the criminal law, since many of the illegal acts of corporations have only civil penalties attached. At the same time, scholars found that they could not draw valid conclusions regarding the sanctioning of corporations unless they studied the operation of the enforcement process.

For these reasons, criminologists turned their attention to the study of regulation and its enforcement. They found that the theoretical approaches used by criminal justice researchers to study the criminal justice system could be adapted to examine the operation of this alternative system of justice.

Models of Regulation

The criminal justice perspective on regulation is only one of four models which have been used by scholars for analyzing and interpreting the operation of regulatory agencies. None of these models provides a complete picture of regulation, because each presents only a slice of reality. Together, however, they complement one another and offer a framework for analyzing regulation.

The Justice Model of Regulation

As noted above, the justice model of regulation utilizes concepts like those used in the study of criminal justice. Within this model, regulation is viewed as a system of social control. Studies of regulation within the justice model describe the processes of investigation, adjudication, and punishment, focusing on issues of discretion, due process, and effectiveness.

The Rational-Legal Model

The rational-legal model of law asserts that law provides a rational and definitive solution to social problems. According to this view, whenever a problem is identified, rational lawmakers create rules to eliminate the problem. The identification of problems is assumed to occur either through consensus within society or through the wisdom of the lawmakers. In the context of regulation, this approach has focused particularly upon the expertise of regulatory administrators and their ability to create rational rules which solve problems. Thus, for example, if scientists have found that a particular food additive causes cancer, regulators are expected to create regulations restricting the use of the additive, applying rational criteria for their decisions. Enforcement is taken for granted as a natural consequence of law and the discovery of a violation, and is viewed as impartial and objective.

The Economic Model of Regulation

Another approach to the study of regulation is the economic model, which examines regulation in terms of the overall efficiency of the economy. The economic model seeks to identify regulatory policies that will maximize social benefits and minimize social costs. A principal tool of the economic model is cost-benefit analysis. Focusing primarily on the rule-making activities of regulatory agencies, the economic model investigates whether regulations create social benefits that outweigh their costs. Within the economic model, maximization of choice is generally preferred over legal controls which constrain choice.

The Conflict Model of Regulation

A fourth model for understanding regulation focuses on the use of the regulatory system for gaining privileges and advantages. Applying a group conflict model of society, this perspective sees regulation as a political tool for assigning rights and responsibilities. Environmentalists, for example, seek regulations which will establish rights to clean air, pure water, and unspoiled wilderness. Their opponents—primarily mining and manufacturing industries—seek regulations that will protect profits and preserve their rights to conduct business where and how they choose. Each group mobilizes power and uses the political arena to influence the regulatory process. The conflict model focuses on issues of power and views all regulatory processes and outcomes in terms of power struggles.

These four models of regulation focus on different, but related, issues. The models are not exclusive of one another, but provide alternative viewpoints for conceptualizing and understanding the regulatory process. Each contributes in its own way to an understanding of the whole.

Conclusion

Criminological studies of the last ten years have demonstrated the serious impact of corporate illegality on our lives, which is estimated to far exceed the costs of conventional crimes (Reiman, 1979; Schrager and Short, 1980). If we are to learn how corporate illegality might be better controlled, we must understand how the regulatory justice system works. At the same time, this system of control should be scrutinized to determine whether it is operating fairly and reasonably, since the system of control that we invent today frequently becomes the problem that needs to be controlled tomorrow.

References

Clinard, Marshall B. and Peter C. Yeager (1980) *Corporate Crime*. New York: The Free Press.

Cressey, Donald R. (1953) *Other People's Money*. New York: Free Press.

Ermann, M. David and Richard J. Lundman (1978) *Corporate and Governmental Deviance: Problems in Organizational Behavior in Contemporary Society*. New York: Oxford University Press.

Geis, Gilbert (1986) "White-Collar Crime: The Heavy Electrical Equipment Antitrust Cases of 1961." In Marshall B. Clinard and Richard Quinney (eds.) *Criminal Behavior Systems: A Typology*. Cincinnati: Anderson Publishing Co.

Geis, Gilbert and Ezra Stotland (1980) *White-Collar Crime: Theory and Research*. Beverly Hills: Sage.

MacDonagh, Oliver (1958) "The Nineteenth-Century Revolution in Government: A Reappraisal." *Historical Journal* 1: 52-67.

Mendeloff, John (1979) *Regulating Safety: A Political and Economic Analysis of the Federal Occupational Safety and Health Program*. Cambridge, MA: MIT Press.

Reiman, Jeffrey (1979) *The Rich Get Richer and the Poor Get Prison*. New York: Wiley.

Schrager, Laura Shill and James F. Short (1980) "How Serious a Crime? Perceptions of Organizational and Common Crimes." In Gilbert Geis and Ezra Stotland (eds.) *White-Collar Crime: Theory and Research.* Beverly Hills: Sage.

Stone, Christopher D. (1975) *Where the Law Ends: The Social Control of Corporate Behavior.* New York: Harper and Row.

_____(1985) "Corporate Regulation: The Place of Social Responsibility." In Brent Fisse and Peter A. French (eds.) *Corrigible Corporations and Unruly Law.* San Antonio: Trinity University Press.

Vogel, David (1981) "The 'New' Social Regulation in Historical and Comparative Perspective." In Thomas K. McGraw (ed.) *Regulation in Perspective: Historical Essays.* Cambridge, MA: Harvard University Press.

Weidenbaum, Murray L. (1977) *Business, Government, and the Public.* Englewood Cliffs, NJ: Prentice-Hall.

Wilson, James Q. (1980) *The Politics of Regulation.* New York: Basic Books.

CHAPTER 2

Regulation in Our Lives

Regulation is a pervasive phenomenon in modern society, visible in the form of scores of local, state, and federal regulatory agencies as well as armies of regulators making rules, investigating for violations, and enforcing regulations. Regulation has brought government into our homes, into factories and stores, and into schools and offices. Virtually every aspect of our lives is touched by regulation. The quality of the food we eat, the purity of the air we breathe, the content of the programs we watch on television, the safety of our workplaces, the kinds of cars we drive—all have been influenced or controlled by regulation. The increasing recognition of the enormous impact of regulation has made it one of the major social and political issues of the 1980s. Yet all too often, those touched by regulation remain unclear about what regulation is supposed to do.

According to the economic model of regulation, the purpose of regulation is to correct "market failures." When, due to inadequate information or the existence of natural monopolies or other imperfections, the free market does not operate at optimal efficiency, economists have frequently argued for government intervention to correct or compensate for these imperfections.

Broadly speaking, the functions of regulation can be divided into two major categories: social control and service. Social control refers to efforts to directly prevent or deter a person or corporation from engaging in activities which have been deemed to be socially harmful. Service refers to regulatory efforts to provide coordination and mediation where these are needed to improve the performance of private individuals, corporations, or markets. Although we will look at these functions separately for the purposes of analysis, these functions are closely related. In fact, when regulation controls one group of people, it often is performing a service for yet another group.

Regulation as Social Control

Frequently, the effects of technological and social changes are not perceived to have any ill effects, or the effects are so taken for granted that

they are not viewed as a "problem." Only when the public, or some important segment of the public, recognizes the effects of "progress" as troublesome do these effects become the subjects of regulation and control
(Spector and Kitsuse, 1973). Thus, periodically, reform movements arise
designed to address these perceived "problems" created by social changes.
Moreover, the solutions which these reformers devise are directly related to
their perceptions of the causes of the "problem."

According to the conflict model, whether a problem is recognized as
requiring government control depends upon the balance of interests that
are affected. If powerful groups in society are affected by the problem,
those groups will use their power to influence legislators to regulate the
troublesome behavior. On the other hand, if powerful groups would be
hurt by regulation, they may mobilize their power to prevent the creation of
regulation, or to frustrate enforcement, or even to repeal existing regulation.

In contrast, the rational-legal model and the economic model tend to
focus on broad societal interests rather than on the conflicts between
groups in society. These models suggest that regulation will be created to
control problems when it is rational or efficient to do so. In the lexicon of
economics, this means that regulation will (or should) be created when government control will correct for market imperfections that decrease the efficiency of the economy as a whole, regardless of whether it is the behavior of
powerful or of powerless groups that must be controlled. The market imperfections that correspond to the control functions of regulation include
information shortages, the existence of externalities, and the existence of
monopolies.

Information Shortages

Economic theory assumes that consumers have complete knowledge in
the marketplace. Only with complete knowledge can consumers behave rationally, as economic theory assumes. If consumers lack complete information, their choices will not be economically rational or efficient.

For example, if a consumer is buying a refrigerator, she may be interested in how energy efficient the refrigerator is. Although she cannot determine energy efficiency by looking at the refrigerator, lacking any information on the energy consumption of alternative models, she may assume that
those models with a larger capacity will be more inefficient to operate. If,
however, the larger models are equipped with more efficient motors and insulation, her assumption will be incorrect—and she will choose a refrigerator
that is actually less efficient than what she had wanted.

Information shortages exist with respect to many products and services, and many different kinds of information. Sometimes what is lacking is price information, at other times it is information about performance, while at still other times the information that is lacking relates to hidden hazards or side-effects connected with the product. And again, the problem with information shortages, from an economic perspective, is interference with the rational behavior of consumers. If consumers had full information, they would make different choices.

Regulations are frequently designed to correct for naturally occurring shortages of information. Manufacturers of insulation, refrigerators, air conditioners, and automobiles are required to provide information concerning the energy efficiency of their products. Drug manufacturers are required to disclose any side effects of the drugs they sell. Offerors of equity stock must disclose information relating to the financial performance of the corporation. Lenders are required to provide full information about the credit terms under which they are lending money to consumers.

Although economic efficiency is the rationale for regulations requiring disclosure of information, these regulations have come under criticism. It has been suggested that current mandatory disclosure regulations require businesses to disclose more information than consumers want or can rationally use. According to Bardach and Kagan (1982: 251), "there seems to be a pervasive tendency for consumer advocates, legislators, and regulators...to underestimate the extent to which market and private sources produce and disseminate generally adequate amounts of protective information."

In addition, technical problems arise in legislating how the information must be provided. Thus, even seemingly "technical" determinations, such as whether the market provides sufficient information to promote economic efficiency, is subject to judgment. And since there are costs attached to providing additional information, the conflict model suggests that those groups who would be compelled to provide the additional information have an interest in persuading lawmakers that more information will not change the decisions consumers make.

Externalities

Economists use the term "externalities" to refer to the effects that one's behavior has on third parties. An action possesses positive externalities when the transactions between two parties produce unintended benefits for a third party. For example, when I pay a painter to come and paint the outside of my house, it not only increases the value of my own property, but it produces the positive externality of improving the neighborhood and thereby increases the value of my neighbor's property as well.

An action possesses negative externalities when the transactions between two parties impose costs on third parties. Many regulations are aimed at controlling negative externalities. A classic example is the factory that dumps waste in the river. The pollution of the Grand Calumet River is just one of many real-life examples.

In the early years of the nineteenth century, U.S. Steel built a plant at Gary, Indiana, along the Grand Calumet River. The Gary works used the river as a "free disposal system for unwanted chemical effluents," byproducts of the steel production process (Greer, 1980: 170). Before the construction of the steel plant, the river had been enjoyed by local anglers as well as by commercial fishermen as a source of whitefish and sturgeon. By the 1940s, the effluent from the plant had made the water too polluted to sustain fish and made the river "entirely unfit for any recreational activity" (Greer, 1980: 171). Because U.S. Steel was able to use the river as a "free disposal system," it did not have to pay to have its wastes removed. This cost savings was passed on to the purchasers of U.S. Steel products in the form of lower prices and to the stockholders in the company in the form of higher dividends, and maybe even to workers in the form of higher wages.

But the costs did not disappear just because U.S. Steel was able to avoid paying them. The costs were borne by the fishermen whose livelihood was destroyed, by the residents of the Gary area, who lost a valuable recreational resource, and by the residents of Chicago, whose water supply was affected by the discharges from the Gary plant.

One of the oldest legal means of controlling externalities is private civil suits, in which the plaintiff complains that he or she has lost some valuable right as a result of the action of the defendant. Although the civil suit remains a potent weapon to compensate for externalities, in recent years regulation has been relied on more and more to prevent negative externalities. So, for example, pollution regulations control the kind and amount of wastes that manufacturers may dump into the water (or air) and force them to bear the cost of disposing of their wastes in ways that will not affect third parties. By absorbing these costs, a market imperfection is corrected; that is, the price of the goods produced will reflect the full cost of production, including the costs of eliminating wastes.

Once again, however, it is important to note the predictions of the conflict model, which suggests that regulations preventing externalities will be created only if the third parties bearing the costs possess more political power than the groups which have benefited from the externality. Where the economic model suggests that these decisions are (or should) be made rationally, according to economic efficiency, the conflict model suggests that these decisions will be made politically, regardless of what is morally fair or economically efficient.

Monopolies

Another market imperfection that usually requires regulation to control, rather than to coordinate the provision of services, is the existence of monopolies. Monopolies exist when there are too few producers of a good, which decreases consumers' options. This situation increases the market power of the producers, who are able to increase prices above the level that would exist if there were many producers of the same good. In economists' terms, monopoly is bad because it is economically inefficient.

Regulation has been used for decades as a means of preventing monopolies or even of breaking up existing monopolies. Antitrust legislation was passed around the turn of the century to control the large "trusts," particularly companies like Standard Oil, which were viewed as having too much economic power to be good for the economy as a whole. Antitrust law was passed in an effort to prevent large producers from squeezing out smaller ones. In addition to various state and federal statutes, the Federal Trade Commission was given responsibility for "withstalling mergers or acquisitions that might substantially lessen competition or tend to create a monopoly" (Katzman, 1980: 154).

Although the economists' arguments about the dangers of monopoly have no doubt been an important influence on the development of antitrust regulation, historians have noted that political concerns were important in shaping antitrust laws and the administration of antitrust regulation (see, for example, Hofstadter, 1955; Kolko, 1963; 1965; Weinstein, 1968). Antitrust legislation was sought primarily by farmers and small businessmen seeking protection from competition with corporate giants (Knepper, 1986). In addition to the economic arguments against monopoly, the public and many politicians distrusted the amalgamation of power that large corporations represented. As Robert Katzman (1980) observes:

> Antitrust is a banner under which many march but for quite different reasons: politicians grappling with inflation; consumer groups convinced that large manufacturers charge supranormal prices; populists fearful that corporate giants corrupt the political process; businessmen threatened by the anticompetitive behavior of others; private attorneys dependent on antitrust practice as a source of income; and economists concerned with the welfare costs of monopoly and the estimated consumer gains from its elimination.

Thus, economic efficiency was an argument in favor of antitrust regulation, but was not the sole motivating factor leading to the passage of antitrust legislation.

Regulation as Service

As a system of law, regulation serves obvious social control functions. Less obvious, perhaps, are the many service functions it performs, to which we now turn. The service function that regulation performs is often, but not necessarily, a secondary effect of regulation as social control.   As in the case of the SEC, stability, consumer confidence, and other such benefits were the other side of the regulatory coin, complementing the social control function. Similarly, the Meat Inspection Act of 1906, which was passed to control disgusting and unhealthy practices in the meat industry, also functioned to recapture European markets for American processed meat products (Kolko, 1963).

In addition to providing a service to third parties, who benefit from the control that regulation provides, many regulations provide a service to the regulated firms themselves. For example, the regulation of routes and fares by the Civil Aeronautics Board (CAB) benefited the airline industry at least as much as it controlled the industry. By creating monopolies for airlines over certain routes, regulation insured excellent profit margins, generally promoted the health of the airline industry, and caused large segments of the industry to prosper (Behrman, 1980).

According to the economic model, economic efficiency suffers if: (1) markets for some goods do not exist, (2) the goods are public, or (3) natural monopolies exist. In these instances, regulation may be used to correct the imperfection, and the "regulated" groups in these instances frequently view regulation as a service rather than as control.

Non-existent Markets

Regulation is sometimes used when markets for some goods do not exist, even though the goods themselves are socially beneficial. Economic demand for these goods may not develop because of lack of information, uncertainty in the market, or other reasons.

One remedy that government may pursue when there is no market for a good is to create a market through regulation. These regulations may be designed to provide the needed information, reduce uncertainty, control prices, or otherwise create the conditions under which a market will develop. Regulations may be primarily facilitative, as when the government provides subsidies for the good, or the regulations may be more coercive, as when the government puts controls on the price of the good or requires that consumers purchase the good.

An example of such regulations is the requirement that seatbelts be installed in all automobiles. Within the language of the economic model, the government assessed the benefits of seatbelts and found them to be a social good for which there was inadequate economic demand because consumers lacked information about the benefits of seatbelts. The government then intervened in the marketplace to dictate a market for seatbelts.

Public Goods

A variety of "goods" are considered by economists to be public goods. These are goods which are not normally bought and sold and which are enjoyed by the whole society. The creation of public goods frequently can be attained only through common effort. Some examples include the creation and preservation of wilderness areas, the maintenance of national defense, and the building of flood-control projects. In other cases, natural, unavoidable shortages of a good make the good public in nature. For example, radio frequencies and air space are limited. Nothing that producers do can increase the supply of these goods.

Where a good is public it is common for the government to intervene to facilitate the production of the good or to oversee its distribution. For example, the Forest Service has responsibility for the maintenance of national woodlands. In fulfilling its responsibilities, the Forest Service promulgates regulations pertaining to the fair use of forest lands to ensure maximum public enjoyment and maximum protection of the forests.

Natural Monopolies

Some kinds of goods are called natural monopolies. These are goods which can be most efficiently produced if there is only one supplier. Some of the goods which have been dealt with as natural monopolies include public water supplies, public utilities (electricity and gas), communication networks, such as telephone service and cable television, and transportation networks, such as city bus service.

One of the common responses to the existence of a natural monopoly is to allow a single firm to establish a monopoly in the production and distribution of the good, but to have the monopoly under government regulation. The creation of public service commissions is an example of the attempt of government to control natural monopolies. Because it was considered more efficient for a single company to generate power for a community, rather than establishing a number of competing generating companies, electric companies formed monopolies in particular areas. But to make sure that their prices were fair to consumers, the government imposed regulation on the industry, requiring utility companies to obtain the approval of the public service commission for all price increases. These commissions also had jurisdiction over natural gas and telephone services and rates.

Recently, some economists have argued that not all of the goods which have been treated as natural monopolies are really more efficiently produced under a monopoly system (see, for example, Green, 1973; Kahn, 1970). The realities of administrative rule-making, including delay, inflexibility, lack of information, lack of expertise, politics, and business pressure, combine to make government regulation of these monopolies irrational and often contradictory (Breyer, 1982). In response to these kinds of criticisms, a number of industries have been "deregulated."

One of the lessons that has been learned from the regulation and subsequent deregulation of "natural monopolies" is that when regulation is doing a service to the regulated industry, it may be doing a disservice to the public and to potential competitors of the regulated industry. Unfortunately, regulation is frequently perceived only in terms of social control, as coming from "out there." The fallacy of this perception will be discussed in greater detail in subsequent chapters, but from the perspective of "regulation as service," it must be noted that regulated industries, such as the airline, trucking or telecommunications industries, created regulations in tandem with government regulators. The Civil Aeronautics Board, Interstate Commerce Commission, and Federal Communications Commission were criticized as being too protective of and unduly influenced by the established firms in the industry (Bernstein, 1955; Green, 1973). In this respect, "service" regulations are not externally imposed control but, rather, invited by industry as a means of rationalizing markets to meet their needs. Industry frequently is willing to put up with some degree of external control in exchange for the order, predictability, and economic stability regulation affords.

Targets of Regulation:
Individuals, Corporations, Governments

When people use the term "regulation," they most commonly use it in reference to the regulation of business. While regulations affecting business probably account for the majority of regulation and will be the primary focus of this book, the regulatory form of governmental social control has been applied to other kinds of activities as well. While people tend to think of regulation primarily in terms of the activities of corporations, individuals and governments are frequently subjected to regulation.

Regulating Individuals

The word "business" often conjures images of "big business," of giant corporations with assets of truly mind-boggling proportions. It is important to keep in mind, however, that most businesses are small, often run by one or two individuals. Although small businesses are frequently exempt from regulatory requirements under federal law, small businesses—and the individuals who own them—experience a great deal of regulation under state and local laws. Individuals are the major targets of state and local regulations found in building codes, plumbing codes, and restaurant regulations, to name only a few.

One of the principal forms of regulation is occupational licensing, which affects individuals in diverse occupations, from embalmers to cheesemakers. The number of occupations which were brought under government regulation through the licensing process grew rapidly during the first regulatory spurt of the Progressive Era. The idea of occupational licensing was not new during this period; both England and the American colonies had licensed lawyers. Moreover, discriminatory licensing, such as requiring street peddlers to get a license, thereby protecting local merchants from competition were quite common, despite public acclamations of *laissez-faire* ideology. During the Progressive Era, however, licensing was applied to a number of previously unregulated occupations, starting with the medical professions—doctors, pharmacists, dentists, nurses, and others (Friedman, 1973). Today, dozens of occupations are licensed. There are a variety of reasons for requiring licenses in these diverse areas of activity.

First, licenses may be required in order to establish a set of minimum qualifications for engaging in certain activities. For example, in order to operate a motor vehicle, the state wants to be assured that the driver is able to see, that the driver knows the traffic regulations, and that the driver has an appropriate degree of skill in operating a motor vehicle. Thus, state authorities require prospective drivers to pass a number of examinations to ensure that the driver has the necessary qualifications. The rationale for the qualifications is related to the risk of harm that would be created by having unqualified people engaging in a potentially hazardous activity.

Not all licensing activity is related to safety, however. In some cases the purpose of requiring a license is to regulate competition by controlling how many and which people get an opportunity to operate in a particular field or area. These licenses are meant to be issued according to economic principles in an attempt to stabilize markets and prices.

Another purpose of licenses is to provide a source of revenue for the governmental unit issuing the license. In some cases, the license fee may be set at a level which will offset the costs of the regulatory program. In other cases, the license fee is really a form of taxation, a means of raising revenue over and above the costs of administering the regulatory program.

Yet another function of occupational licensing has been to establish a profession by defining it in the law. Friedman describes the licensing of undertakers, embalmers and funeral directors in this way. According to Friedman (1973: 398), these groups were:

> struggling to define for themselves, and to protect, an area of exclusive business competence. They had many rivals. Doctors embalmed the dead. Clergymen controlled funerals. Many undertakers were part-time funeral directors, who sold coffins and caskets as the mainstay of their business. In the late 1880s, Hudson Samson, president of the Funeral Directors' National Association of the United States, prepared a model legislative act for licensing embalmers. At the same time, Samson tried to uplift the artifacts of professional funerals....It was all part of one general movement, to give tone and economic strength to the occupation, in short, to "professionalize" these doctors of the dead. Samson wanted a law to regulate "the care and burial of the dead the same as there is for the practice of medicine." In 1894, Virginia passed the first licensing law....Thereafter, only registered embalmers could practice the "science of embalming." By 1900, some twenty-four states had passed similar legislation.

Other occupations quickly followed suit. Again, safety was frequently used to justify the need for licensing, but the desire to avoid competition was probably the primary reason that most occupational groups sought the protection of licensing.

Occupational licensing relates to individuals, but only in relation to their business activities. Other regulations are aimed exclusively at individuals. Motor vehicle regulation brings many individuals into contact with the regulatory form of social control. You apply to a regulatory agency for a driver's license. The agency makes rules concerning the operation of motor vehicles, and if you violate the rules, your license may be suspended or revoked by the agency.

Finally, in order to qualify for various government benefits, such as farm subsidies, educational loans, food stamps, unemployment compensation, and small-business loans, individuals must meet a variety of criteria and follow the regulations of the agency administering the benefit. Whether these agencies are properly called "regulatory" has been a topic of debate. Although social control may not be a primary or even an intended function of these agencies, which are principally concerned with the distribution of government benefits, there is no denying that in practice these agencies regulate the behavior of individuals obtaining these benefits (Spector, 1981). If a beneficiary fails to meet one of the requirements or violates any of the rules of the agency, benefits can be suspended or revoked, just as licenses and permits may be revoked.

Regulating Corporations

Most regulatory agencies are involved in activities directly related to the conduct of business. Regulatory agencies have been responsible for setting the rates that may be charged by railroads, trucking firms, airlines, electric utilities, petroleum producers, and banks. Regulatory agencies set up criteria for determining which firms may enter particular lines of enterprise, limiting access to the market in communications, air transportation, and nuclear generation of electricity, among others.

Regulatory agencies set solvency standards for banks and insurance companies to protect depositors and policy-holders. Agencies further attempt to protect the customers of businesses by requiring businesses to disclose certain kinds of information and by requiring that advertising be truthful, fair, and not misleading.

Corporations may also be required to obtain licenses for various activities. For example, licenses are required in order to operate a restaurant, to produce and sell milk for interstate commerce, to manufacture drugs, or to operate a nuclear facility.

As in the case of the regulation of individuals, businesses frequently are subjected to regulation when they apply for various government benefits, such as government contracts, which impose a variety of regulations on government contractors, particularly relating to employment practices. For example, the Walsh-Healey Act prescribes minimum wages, hours, and work conditions for employees of government supply contractors, and the Clean Air Act of 1970 prohibits the awarding of government contracts to any company convicted of a criminal violation of air pollution standards (Weidenbaum, 1977: 123-124).

Other regulatory agencies attempt to prevent the harmful side effects of industrial production. Sanitation in food production, the safety of drugs and food additives, the effectiveness of drugs, the safety of automobiles and of passenger airliners, safety and health in the workplace, the hidden hazards of consumer products, and environmental protection have all become the subjects of regulation.

All of these regulations constrain business, preventing some practices entirely and requiring that others be carried out in specified ways. Production and sale of some products is banned entirely, such as laetrile and DDT. Other products, like certain pesticides or drugs, can be manufactured only by a few firms holding special permits issued by the regulatory agency. Some products, like milk and automobiles, must meet standards of quality or performance.

Finally, in some instances, the structure of the industry itself is regulated. Antitrust regulation is used to prevent firms from obtaining too large a share of the market in a given industry. The Federal Trade Commission may even order business firms to reorganize, to sell subsidiaries, or to dissolve into a number of smaller firms.

Regulating Government

A new development of the 1960s was the regulation of government, usually by a higher level of government. Many of these regulations are associated with the transfer of federal funds to other units of government, such as federal grants-in-aid for education, mass transit, and urban housing. The regulations are intended to guarantee that the funds are used for their intended purposes and that the programs receiving federal funds comply with federal civil rights law and equal opportunity regulations.

Finally, some regulatory agencies police other regulatory agencies. For example, the federal Occupational Safety and Health Administration may certify a state work safety program, allowing the state to take full responsibility for enforcing federal work safety regulations. The federal agency monitors the state program to assure that it meets minimal standards. Similar supervisory relationships exist in other areas of regulation and between state and local governments.

The Pervasiveness of Regulation

Surveying the enormous scope of regulation, it is difficult to escape the conclusion that regulation is indeed pervasive, touching virtually everything a person does. The explosion in regulation has greatly expanded governmental social control. In addition, where once reactive forms of control, like civil suits for damages, were used to control problems like fraudulent real estate sales or job accidents, regulation utilizes more proactive forms of control, including prohibition, licensing, and surveillance. These broadened and intensified control functions make some people worry that governmental control may be spiralling out of our control. Some have raised concern that we should be cautious about government repression in the guise of regulation.

At the same time, however, we have come to expect governmental intervention to protect us from harm and to provide various services and co-ordination in the form of regulation. Indeed, when we hear that some preventable harm has occurred, we often ask why the government failed to act to prevent the harm. For example, when a coal mine explosion occurs, reporters are as apt to question government mine inspectors about their failures as they are to question the mine operators about their responsibility in failing to prevent the explosion.

The expansion of regulation has created, or is the result of, rising expectations of what government is expected to do. Opinion polls consistently show strong public support for health, safety, and environmental regulation (Clinard and Yeager, 1980: 99; League of Women Voters, 1982). Clearly, the majority of Americans view regulation as a legitimate and necessary governmental function. Therefore, regulations are pervasive because our expectations of government are so great. As a result, not only are regulations themselves pervasive, but regulation affects our relationships to government and to one another, changing the nature of the social contract between individuals and government.

The Structure of Regulatory Bureaucracies

To perform the diverse functions outlined above, regulatory agencies are usually organized in one of two ways: as independent agencies or as executive departments (see Figure 2.1). The first independent agencies were created during the late 1800s and were originally viewed as a means of insulating regulatory decision-making from political pressures. Independent agencies were expected to administer regulations impartially, in light of the specialized technical expertise of members of the governing board of the agency.

Independent regulatory agencies are composed of a board or commission whose members typically are appointed by the chief executive (governor or President). Because each member serves a fixed term, the executive is not in direct control of the membership of the board. The board, in turn, is given the authority to function independent of the executive branch. Because of this form of organization, independent agencies have sometimes been referred to as the "fourth branch" of government, since technically these agencies are not part of the legislative, executive, or judicial branches.

Figure 2.1
The Bureaucratic Structure of Key Federal Regulatory Agencies

Independent Agencies:
  Interstate Commerce Commission
  Federal Trade Commission
  Federal Communications Commission
  Securities and Exchange Commission
  National Labor Relations Board
  Board of Governors of the Federal Reserve System
  Nuclear Regulatory Commission
  Consumer Product Safety Commission
  Equal Employment Opportunity Commission

Executive Branch Agencies:
  Food and Drug Administration
  Occupational Safety and Health Administration
  Coal Mine Safety and Health Administration
  Internal Revenue Service
  Immigration and Naturalization Service
  Forest Service
  Environmental Protection Agency
  National Highway Traffic and Safety Administration

Source: Florence Heffron with Neil McFeeley, The Administrative Regulatory Process. New York: Longman, 1983.

Executive branch agencies, in contrast, are directly under the authority of the executive. Heads of executive branch agencies may be appointed directly by the chief executive or by a cabinet member. This form of organization affords the executive greater control over the activities of the agency.

Within the political science literature, one can find a great deal of discussion, debate, and research concerning the differences between independent regulatory agencies and executive branch agencies. Although, initially, scholars believed that the independent agency would be more insulated than an executive agency from political pressures, subsequent research has shown that although the process of political influence is different, independent agencies are just as much influenced by "politics" as executive department agencies. While independent agencies offer greater stability, since their management does not shift with every new election of a chief executive, political influence is exerted through budget processes, legislative oversight, and clientele groups.

Functions of Regulatory Agencies

Whether organized as an independent agency or under the authority of the chief executive, regulatory agencies perform a variety of functions, spanning the three primary functions of government: legislative, executive, and judicial functions. In most cases, all three of these functions are performed by a single agency, although in some cases one or more of these functions have been housed in separate agencies (see, e.g., the Occupation Safety and Health Administration and the Occupational Safety and Health Review Commission).

Because most regulatory agencies perform all three basic functions of government, a long-term legal debate has been fought concerning the "separation of powers" doctrine (Heffron and McFeeley, 1983). The framers of the Constitution believed that by separating the three basic powers of government among three different branches of government, the people would be protected from the tyranny of an all-powerful government through the checks and balances created by the separation of powers. As Heffron and McFeeley (1983: 40) point out, the concept of separation of powers

> is implied by the grants of power in Articles I, II, and III. Article I begins, "all legislative powers herein granted shall be vested in the Congress of the United States..." Article II states, "The executive power shall be vested in the President...," while the third Article states, "The judicial power of the United States shall be vested in one supreme court, and in such inferior courts..."

Nonetheless, regulatory agencies commonly possess all three powers, constitutional provisions and philosophical tradition notwithstanding. Through a number of legal maneuvers the courts have affirmed the tripartite powers of regulatory agencies. Thus, although the separation of powers is still a basis for challenging some regulatory actions, there is no longer any serious controversy surrounding the basic notion of agencies fulfilling all three functions.

Rule-making

Congress and state legislatures have delegated to regulatory agencies the authority to make rules concerning particular regulatory problems.[1] This delegation of legislative authority to regulatory agencies is based upon the presumption that regulatory officials possess expertise in relation to regulatory problems and that they are best able to determine what rules are necessary to achieve the goals of regulation. Through their rule-making powers, regulatory agencies determine the behaviors which will be prohibited and penalized. Although the legislative branch will usually specify the penalties that may be applied to violations of regulations, it is the regulatory agency that decides precisely which behaviors will receive these penalties. Thus, the legislature sets the broad parameters within which an agency may make rules, but allows the agency to "fill in the blanks."

For example, rather than Congress passing legislation defining the specific safety standards which employers must achieve in the workplace, Congress delegates this power to the Occupational Safety and Health Administration (OSHA). OSHA, in turn, creates specific rules relating to a broad variety of potential hazards in particular types of workplaces.

Through the rule-making powers of regulatory agencies, it is possible to develop laws which are more specific than the vague pronouncements of Congress or state legislatures. To use the OSHA example, rather than Congress merely passing a law that all machinery must be guarded, OSHA is able to develop specific rules describing the types of guards that are required on particular types of machinery.

Administration

The executive functions of regulatory agencies involve a variety of different types of activities. Administration is the process of applying general rules or standards to particular cases. Regulatory administration involves granting licenses, approving the design or formulation of products, and setting prices for various commodities. Administration also takes the form of investigating for violations of regulations and enforcing regulatory rules.

Our primary interest in regulatory administration as it relates to corporate illegality focuses on the investigatory and enforcement functions of regulatory agencies. Analagous to police agencies, regulatory agencies must discover violations, collect evidence to substantiate any legal action taken in response to the violation, and initiate legal action before any penalties can be imposed. Like police, regulatory officials exercise a great deal of discretion in enforcing regulations.

Adjudication

In addition to deciding when legal action is necessary and desirable and initiating the appropriate legal action, regulatory agencies are also vested with the authority to complete some types of legal action. Suspension and revocation of licenses and permits, seizures of products which violate standards, closure of facilities that do not meet regulatory standards, and administrative imposition of fines are all actions which may be taken by the regulatory agency following internal procedures, without having to go to court or obtain authority from any other external source. In some cases, penalties may be imposed before any fact-finding hearing has been held, though the violator may request a hearing after the fact to challenge the agency's action.

Conclusion

The subsequent chapters of this book will describe how regulatory agencies actually carry out the functions just described. Given the pervasiveness of regulation, how the regulatory system works necessarily affects each of us. The principal aim of this book is to describe how the regulatory system works and *why* it works that way. If we understand how the regulatory system operates, we may be better able to exercise control over it and its effects on our lives.

Notes

[1] The doctrine of the non-delegability of powers was another constitutional objection to administrative rule-making. This doctrine is described in greater detail in Chapter 3.

References

Bardach, Eugene and Robert A. Kagan (1982) *Going by the Book: The Problem of Regulatory Unreasonableness*. Philadelphia: Temple University Press.

Behrman, Bradley (1980) "Civil Aeronautics Board." In James Q. Wilson (ed.) *The Politics of Regulation*. New York: Basic Books.

Bernstein, Marver (1955) *Regulating Business by Independent Commission.* Princeton, NJ: Princeton University Press.

Breyer, Stephen (1982) *Regulation and its Reform.* Cambridge, MA: Harvard University Press.

Clinard, Marshall B. and Peter C. Yeager (1980) *Corporate Crime.* New York: Free Press.

Friedman, Lawrence (1973) *A History of American Law.* New York: Simon and Schuster.

Green, Mark (1973) *The Monopoly Makers: Ralph Nader's Study Group Report on Regulation and Competition.* New York: Grossman.

Greer, Edward (1980) "And Filthy Flows the Calumet." In Mark Green and Robert Massie, Jr. (eds.) *The Big Business Reader: Essays on Corporate America.* New York: Pilgrim Press.

Heffron, Florence with Neil McFeeley (1983) *The Administrative Regulatory Process.* New York: Longman.

Hofstadter, Richard (1955) *The Age of Reform.* New York: Vintage Books.

Kahn, Alfred E. (1970) *The Economics of Regulation: Principles and Institutions.* New York: Wiley and Sons.

Katzman, Robert (1980) "Federal Trade Commission." In James Q. Wilson (ed.) *The Politics of Regulation.* New York: Basic Books.

Knepper, Paul (1986) "A Dialectical View of Economic Regulation: The Origins of Antitrust Law and the Early History of its Enforcement." Unpublished manuscript, University of Wisconsin—Milwaukee.

Kolko, Gabriel (1963) *The Triumph of Conservatism.* Glencoe, IL: Free Press.

_____(1965) *Railroads and Regulation: 1877-1916.* Princeton: Princeton University Press.

League of Women Voters (1983) *News Release: League of Women Voters Releases New Poll on Regulatory Process.* Washington, D.C.: League of Women Voters.

Spector, Malcolm (1981) "Beyond Crime: Seven Methods to Control Troublesome Rascals." In H. Laurence Ross (ed.) *Law and Deviance.* Beverly Hills: Sage.

Spector, Malcolm and John I. Kitsuse (1973) "Social Problems: A Re-formulation." *Social Problems* 21: 145-159.

Weidenbaum, Murray L. (1977) *Business, Government, and the Public.* Englewood Cliffs, NJ: Prentice-Hall.

Weinstein, James (1968) *The Corporate Ideal in the Liberal State: 1900-1918.* Boston: Beacon Press.

CHAPTER 3

Rule-making and Regulatory Effectiveness

With the revolution in government that created the regulatory justice system, a new variety of law developed: administrative law. Administrative law defines the powers of regulatory agencies and the procedures they must follow in carrying out their functions. Within the limits set by constitutional and statutory law, regulatory agencies create rules which specify regulatory requirements.

Administrative law is a vast and complex field. It is not within the scope of this book to provide a detailed study of administrative law. Rather, we offer a survey of some of the key provisions of administrative law as they relate to the activities of regulatory agencies.

The Delegation of Legislative Powers

Early in the evolution of the regulatory form of social control, legal scholars debated the constitutionality of the "quasi-legislative" powers granted to regulatory agencies. One legal challenge to the agencies' rule-making power concerned the "separation of powers," discussed in Chapter Two. Another challenge asserted that it was unconstitutional for Congress to delegate its legislative power to an administrative agency.

The basis for this constitutional challenge to regulatory rule-making lay in the common law doctrine of the non-delegability of powers. According to this doctrine, a power that has been delegated may not be re-delegated by the person (or body) to whom the power was first delegated. Thus, since the Constitution delegated legislative power to the Congress, Congress in turn could not re-delegate legislative power to another person or governmental body.

The Supreme Court has upheld the doctrine of non-delegability consistently, beginning in 1831 and continuing to the present (Heffron and McFeeley, 1983). In a sense, however, the legal fight over delegation of powers is an example of winning the battle but losing the war. In spite of regular and consistent Supreme Court support for the doctrine of non-delegability of powers, Congress has continued to grant rule-making power to regulatory agencies, and these grants of rule-making power have, one way or another, been permitted by the very same Court that has held that legislative powers may not be delegated. Through hair-splitting logic, and sometimes no logic at all, the Supreme Court has managed to uphold non-delegability at the same time that it has reaffirmed specific grants of rule-making power.[1]

An example of how the Supreme Court has managed to uphold the non-delegability doctrine at the same time that it upholds the power of regulatory agencies to make essentially legislative decisions is found in the case of *United States v. Grimaud*. In this 1911 Supreme Court decision, the Court held that regulatory agencies are merely "filling in the details" of statutes when they create administrative regulations. In the process, however, regulatory agencies can decide that some behaviors are going to be crimes.

A statute passed around the turn of the century authorized the Secretary of Agriculture to protect the national forests by making rules and regulations governing the use of the forests. Within the same statute, Congress declared that violation of any such rule or regulation promulgated by the Secretary of Agriculture would be a crime. Subsequent to the passage of this statute, the Secretary of Agriculture promulgated a regulation requiring a permit to graze sheep on forest lands.

Grimaud, a sheep-herder, was caught grazing his sheep without a permit and was indicted for the crime of violating the Secretary's regulation. When Grimaud was convicted, he appealed the conviction, eventually taking the issue to the Supreme Court. The issue before the Supreme Court was whether Congress had unconstitutionally delegated power to the Secretary of Agriculture to create a crime.

The Supreme Court held that this was not a delegation of power to create crimes, since it was Congress, and not the Secretary, who decided that all violations of regulations would be crimes. According to the Supreme Court, all the Secretary did was to "fill in the details" of the general congressional mandate to protect forest lands. As long as the rule falls within the mandate, no constitutional problem arises.

The *Grimaud* case presents only one of the theories the Court has used to uphold regulatory rule-making (see Heffron and McFeeley, 1983: 30-43). Thus, while the legal issue of delegation of powers is from time to time raised as a means of challenging and overturning a specific regulatory rule, the general power of regulatory agencies to make rules is no longer seriously disputed.[2]

Of greater contemporary concern are the procedures agencies follow in promulgating new regulations. Regulations are law, with the same legal authority as laws created through the legislative process. Heavy penalties can be exacted from those who violate regulatory rules. Therefore, anyone whose interests are likely to be affected by a new regulation has an interest in having those interests considered by the agency before it issues a new rule.

Administrative Law and the Rule-making Process

Both constitutional and statutory laws control the procedures regulatory agencies follow in promulgating regulations. First and foremost, rule-making procedures must meet the standards of due process. Beyond that, agencies may be required to follow either the formal or informal rule-making procedures of the Administrative Procedures Act, or similar state statutes. Finally, in some cases the agency's enabling statute mandates additional procedures which the agency must follow in rule-making.

The due process clause of the Fourth and Fourteenth Amendments to the Constitution establishes the minimum standards for fair procedures in administrative rule-making. In general, courts have held that due process requires that the government give notice of its intent to promulgate a new rule, that it provide an opportunity for all affected parties to be heard, and that the decision be made in an impartial way.

While these requirements set the minimum for fair rule-making, the due process clause and court decisions interpreting it are vague and non-specific. Thus, an agency considering rule-making may be unable to determine whether the due process clause requires a hearing or whether receiving written comments from affected parties is sufficient to meet the requirement that there be an opportunity to be heard.

More specific instructions are provided through administrative procedures acts at the federal and state levels. These laws were passed during the 1940s and 1950s to make the rule-making process more fair and more consistent from one agency to another. The federal Administrative Procedures Act was passed in 1946 and was used as a model for many state provisions.

The federal act provides two different sets of rule-making procedures: "formal rule-making" and "informal rule-making." Formal rule-making is required only where Congress has clearly indicated that rules are to be made "on the record after an opportunity for an agency hearing..." (Administrative Procedures Act, 1946). Formal rule-making is an adversarial type of hearing procedure in which evidence is submitted. The decision of the impartial hearing officer must be made exclusively on the record of testimony and other evidence submitted during the hearing. *Ex parte* (or "off-the-record") communications are expressly forbidden. These procedures are designed to mimic the adversarial court process, in which opposing parties are given an opportunity to hear and respond to the opposing sides' arguments and in which the decision is based solely on the evidence actually submitted at the hearing. Formal rule-making is currently required, by statute, for sixteen federal agencies (Heffron and McFeeley, 1983: 236).

Informal rule-making is much less cumbersome than the adversarial procedures required by formal rule-making and is also by far the more common method used by regulatory agencies. The requirements include (Heffron and McFeeley, 1983: 237):

1. Notice of the proposed rule-making published in the Federal Register, including a statement of the general substance of the proposed rule and the rule-making procedures that will be followed.

2. An opportunity for interested parties to provide either oral or written comments.

3. A general statement of the basis and purpose of the final rule.

4. Publication of the final rule at least 30 days before its effective date.

No hearing is required and there is no explicit ban on *ex parte* communications.

In addition to these two sets of rule-making procedures found in the Administrative Procedures Act, Congress occasionally mandates special or additional rule-making requirements in the enabling statute for an agency. For example, in a number of cases Congress has specified that rule-making may proceed through the informal process of the Administrative Procedures Act, unless an interested party specifically requests a hearing. The creation of these hybrid procedures has greatly eliminated the hoped-for consistency of rule-making procedures from one agency to another. Thus, learning the kind of rule-making procedures an agency must follow requires a close reading of the agency's enabling statute.

According to the rational-legal model, these procedural requirements should provide an opportunity for all those affected by the regulation to provide relevant information and to express their views and respond to information and opinions submitted by their opponents. After considering information brought forward by the interested parties, the regulatory agency is supposed to promulgate a rule which, in its expert judgment, conforms to the intent of Congress expressed in the enabling statute.

As students of the law and society are quite aware, however, a wide chasm often separates theory and practice. In practice, regulatory rule-makers are not always impartial experts (Miles and Bhambri, 1983: 19). In practice, rather than considering the evidence and coming to a reasoned decision, rule-making is influenced by direct and indirect lobbying and political pressures. In practice, some affected groups consistently dominate the rule-making process, while others are not represented at all.

The Politics of Regulatory Rule-making

Although the law makes a presumption that all interested parties have an equal opportunity to participate, the realities of regulatory rule-making are often quite different. To participate effectively in the regulatory process requires more than writing a letter to the regulatory agency expressing one's views on a proposed rule. Rather, to effectively participate requires an organized, sustained effort involving numerous contacts with regulatory officials, and with those who wield influence with regulatory officials. It frequently requires enormous quantities of information about the projected effects of the regulation, which can only be obtained through vast amounts of research. Historically, with the exception of the era of the 1970s, only the regulated industries have been sufficiently motivated to engage in such an organized effort to influence the outcome of the rule-making process.

The reasons for this can be found in the way in which the effects of regulation are typically distributed. Most areas of regulation deal with harms having effects that are highly diffused, or spread out among a large number of people. For example, acts in restraint of trade, such as price-fixing, and other anti-competitive practices regulated by the FTC, may cause economic harm to consumers that totals billions of dollars each year (Clinard and Yeager, 1980: 8). Even if such practices cost each consumer several hundred dollars each year, consumers would not readily notice the harm because it is spread out over hundreds of purchases. Thus, a person may end up spending a few more cents on each can of soup or a few more dollars on each pair of pants he buys, but these harms go unnoticed by the consumer. Although the consumer may be outraged by price-gouging, and firmly support government efforts to curb such practices, the impact of the harm is so diffused that it is not felt in a way that is likely to motivate the consumer to become actively involved in regulatory politics. Similar observations could be made in relation to public utility regulation, banking and securities regulations, and insurance regulation.

The same is true of regulations concerning health, safety, and the environment. Greater public involvement has been observed in relation to these kinds of regulations than has been the case with economic regulation. Nonetheless, the public's motivation to become involved in efforts to influence the rule-making process are attenuated by the remote nature of the harms. A chemical in the water is expected to cause 1000 excess cancer deaths in twenty years. Since each individual continues to have only a small chance of being one of the unlucky few stricken by cancer, and since even that harm will not occur for another twenty years, the harm is too remote to serve as a source of sustained political action.

The diffuse and remote nature of the harms, and the public's lack of motivation, is in sharp contrast to the direct and immediate impact of regulation on regulated businesses, resulting in strong motivation to become involved in the rule-making process. Some examples from recent regulatory history illustrate these observations.

The FTC and Funeral Regulation

During the late 1960s and early 1970s, the Federal Trade Commission became more activist and interventionist than it had been during most of its seventy-year history. Up until this period of time, the Commission had not initiated any strong consumer protection rules, and Commission actions were rarely controversial.

As a consequence of the growing consumer movement in the 1960s and appointments of staunch consumer advocates to key positions during the Carter administration, the FTC began to challenge long-standing business practices in the advertising, life insurance, breakfast cereal, pharmaceuticals, and funeral industries (Pertschuk, 1982: 54). The FTC charged that various practices in these industries were unfair or involved deceptive advertising.

Michael Pertschuk, chairman of the FTC during this time, offers a vivid picture of how affected businesses seek to influence agency rule-making. A closer look at just one of the FTC's rule-making initiatives, the funeral disclosure rule, illustrates the pressures that are funneled from the regulated industry through Congress to the agency.

The FTC first proposed a rule relating to the funeral industry in August of 1975. The rule worked its way through the FTC's rule-making procedures, undergoing a number of revisions to narrow and focus its scope. By November 1979, the proposed rule contained four basic provisions prohibiting funeral directors from lying to clients about legal requirements, requiring them to answer reasonable questions over the telephone, prohibiting them from requiring expensive caskets for cremation, and requiring funeral directors make available an itemized price list, rather than giving prices only for funeral packages. In economic terms, this rule would have corrected a market imperfection created by funeral directors who were unwilling to make relevant information available to customers.

By the time the full commission had arrived at this relatively modest proposal, the funeral industry had been mobilized to action by the threatened regulatory intervention. Long-standing industry marketing practices were under attack, and the profitability of the industry was at stake. Under the new rules, funeral directors feared, customers might begin to select less expensive funerals in place of more expensive funeral packages that were a mainstay of the funeral business.

Funeral directors went on the offensive to defeat the rule. Their strategy was to lobby Congress. Congress, in turn, could influence the actions of the FTC in a number of ways. Through the Congress' authority to establish the budget for regulatory agencies, including the FTC, members of Congress could warn the agency that continuation of the funeral cost-disclosure rule could result in congressional cut-backs of the agency's budget. Congress also could threaten oversight hearings into the agency's activities, draining off agency resources and bringing critical scrutiny to every agency action. Another source of control lay in Congress' power to amend the enabling legislation, narrowing the agency's authority to exclude certain industries or types of businesses, such as the funeral industry. Finally, because of special provisions in the law relating to the FTC, Congress could veto particular agency rules. Thus, Congress was in a position to directly countermand the agency's own rule-making, as well as being able to exert indirect pressure through subtle, and not so subtle, threats of budget cuts and investigations.

When the funeral industry initially started its campaign against the FTC, it met little opposition. Moreover, as Pertschuk (1982: 60) points out:

> It is, of course, unsurprising that outraged or fearful businessmen and their workers and dependent suppliers within a congressman's district can gain his undivided attention. There is nothing subtle about the threat that the congressman will be held personally accountable at the polls for any regulatory action that adversely affects a firm or its workers. No congressman needs to be told that a funeral director whose customers begin to select $350 funerals in place of $3,500 funeral packages because of a mandatory FTC price-list disclosure rule supported by his congressman will remember nothing else as the next election approaches, while citizen consumers, even those who may benefit, remain blissfully unaware of the rule *or* the vote.

The key here is particularly found in the ignorance and non-involvement of the public which is most likely to benefit from the rule. This public ignorance and inactivity, in contrast to the letters, mailgrams, and personal lobbying of members of Congress by the industry, created an impression for members of Congress that there was a groundswell of opinion against the rule-making efforts of the FTC. As Senator John Danforth commented to Pertschuk, "Everywhere I go in Missouri, to every Rotary and Kiwanis luncheon, all I hear are complaints about the FTC" (Pertschuk, 1982: 62). In the absence of any evidence that there was an active constituency for the proposed rules, Congress was inclined to follow industry's lead and restrain the actions of the FTC.

This is not to say that there was no lobbying in support of the funeral cost-disclosure rule. A coalition of consumer advocates, labor and the elderly began to make their views known to Congress. Their presence and active lobbying served at least to demonstrate enough support for the FTC rule to slow down the defection of congressmen sympathetic to the efforts of the FTC. Indeed, after the House voted to kill the funeral rule, the elderly began to write their congressmen in sufficient numbers "that legislators began to sense that a vote for the friendly local funeral director might not be entirely without cost" (Pertschuk, 1982: 101).

As Pertschuk's account of the siege of the FTC makes clear, the extent to which interest groups organize and participate in regulatory politics is a major influence on the directions agency rule-making will take. Except for the period of the late 1960s and early 1970s, when the Nader consumer movement and the environmental movement served to bring pro-regulation voices into prominence, the normal situation is for regulatory agencies, and their legislative overseers, to be highly aware of industry concerns and interests, but for the interests of consumers or the public to remain unheard, unnoticed, and unrepresented in the rule-making process.

The Civil Aeronautics Board

Another example of the ability of industry to influence the rule-making process is found in the history of the Civil Aeronautics Board (CAB), an agency which has now been dissolved as part of the deregulatory effort begun during the Ford administration. Prior to deregulation, which was done largely to promote the interests of consumers, the CAB operated to benefit airline companies, particularly the larger, established firms. The history of the CAB is ably described by Bradley Behrman (1980: 75-120).

The CAB was created during the New Deal Era. During this time the reigning ideology held that industry needed both to be restrained and protected. Through a system of regulation, government could protect industry from ruinous competition at the same time that it protected consumers from price-gouging by powerful corporations (Breyer, 1982: 29). The fledgling airline industry appeared to New Deal reformers to be just the target for government intervention. "Between 1935 and 1938, domestic airline operations grew 46 percent in plane-miles flown and more than doubled in available seat-miles and revenue passenger-miles. Passenger revenues grew more than 80 percent and total revenues almost 75 percent" (Behrman, 1980: 82). Nonetheless, the airline industry as a whole was losing money, as operating expenses outstripped the rise in revenues. Against this backdrop, "arguments about the dangers of destructive competition also served as a public-interest rationale for airlines to use in trying to convince Congress to protect them from *all* competition" (Behrman, 1980: 81).

Industry got its way in 1938 with the passage of the Civil Aeronautics Act. The Act gave a new independent agency, the Civil Aeronautics Board, the power to issue "certificates," which were permits to operate certain flights at a specified fare. A grandfather provision granted certificates automatically to airlines that had either mail contracts or that had provided regular service for the four months preceding the effective date of the act. In issuing new certificates, the CAB was directed to issue a certificate if it found the applicant "fit, willing, and able" to perform the transportation service and if the transportation service was "required by the public convenience and necessity."

The Act also provided guidelines which the CAB was to follow in setting fares, but the guidelines were vague and frequently contradictory. CAB members would find themselves having to choose between rates that would protect the airline companies and rates that would be "at the lowest cost" (Behrman, 1980: 86). The CAB dealt with these ambiguities by favoring established airline companies. It refused to allow new carriers to establish routes that would compete with established carriers, or for established carriers to offer new routes that would compete with an existing route of another carrier.

While economic wisdom at this time probably supported this approach, the policies of the CAB were also supported by industry influence. The existing carriers spent substantial resources "trying to shape CAB policy through such means as direct lobbying before CAB members and congressmen, rewards to sympathetic congressmen in the form of campaign contributions and votes, and punishments of hostile congressmen through the channeling of funds and votes to opposing candidates" (Behrman, 1980: 89).

While industry was benefiting from the financial stability created by CAB policies, its effects on consumers went unnoticed. No organized groups opposed the policies of the CAB. Consequently, virtually all of the information that CAB members obtained about the airline industry came from the established airlines themselves. This situation continued with little change until shortly before the movement for deregulating the airlines emerged.

The examples from the FTC and the CAB both relate to economic regulation, concerning fair business practices and the correction of supposed market imperfections. One might question whether the public is as quiescent when problems of health and safety are at issue. The following example about rule-making at the Environmental Protection Agency (EPA) shows that despite a generally stronger public awareness of the activities of health and safety regulatory agencies, the domination of the rule-making process by industry representatives is still the rule.

EPA and the Banning of Aldrin/Dieldrin

In 1971, the Environmental Protection Agency initiated proceedings to ban aldrin/dieldrin, a pair of chemically related pesticides used primarily on corn crops. Aldrin/dieldrin was manufactured in the United States exclusively by the Shell Oil Company from 1952 to 1977 (Epstein, 1979: 252). Although aldrin/dieldrin sales peaked in 1966, at 22 million pounds sold, it remained one of the largest selling pesticides, ranking sixth in all U.S. pesticide sales in 1972 (Epstein, 1980: 252).

Nonetheless, evidence was mounting that aldrin/dieldrin were dangerous carcinogens. Although the original tests conducted by Shell to test carcinogenicity had resulted in somewhat equivocal findings, reexamination of the data indicated that aldrin/dieldrin was indeed a cancer-causing pesticide. On the basis of this evidence, EPA initiated action to ban aldrin/dieldrin in the United States.

The Shell Oil Company strongly resisted this effort. The economic impact of the ban on Shell profits would be enormous. As a result, Shell fought hard to resist the regulatory efforts of the EPA, "dragging out the proceedings over 1,700 days" (Epstein, 1979: 259). While Shell used every legal tool available to it to drag out the proceedings, it earned profits of $10 million from the continued sale of aldrin/dieldrin. These profits easily offset the approximately $1 million in legal fees and other additional costs that it incurred, such as hiring consultants and commissioning more studies.

For example, Shell commissioned studies which it used to try to interpret away the EPA's finding of carcinogenicity. Shell retained the services of an "impressive array" of academic consultants, who attempted to refute the results of animal tests. In addition to its submission of test data and expert opinion, Shell also had powerful friends in Congress (Epstein, 1979).

Epstein (1979: 270) summarizes the results of the EPA's efforts to ban aldrin/dieldrin this way:

The success of the regulatory proceedings against [aldrin/dieldrin], resulting in their 1975 ban on the grounds of imminent carcinogenic hazard, was due to the combined efforts of a public interest group and the EPA's Office of General Counsel aided by a small team of independent experts. These were pitted against the massive legal and scientific resources of Shell and the USDA, which supported Shell's position, aided by the politically powerful Southern congressional network and the EPA's own Office of Pesticide Programs, which was hostile to the proceedings.

Once again, we see that regulatory action becomes highly politicized and that industry interests are likely to hold sway unless pro-regulation opponents organize effectively to create some countervailing pressure on the agency and congressional representatives. Even where such an organized opposition exists, wide differences in resources between industry and pro-regulation groups hamper the effectiveness of pro-regulation efforts. As in this example, although Shell Oil Company did not have unlimited resources, its substantial profits from the continued sale of the pesticides not only created the economic incentive to stall banning of the product, these profits served to underwrite the costs of their efforts. Pro-regulatory groups are in a much less advantageous position.

This example also highlights the technical complexity of regulatory issues. In this example, Shell depended on scientific consultants to argue against the ban on aldrin/dieldrin. Even highly motivated citizens can be discouraged from participating in rule-making when a high degree of expertise is needed to assess the meaning of the evidence submitted. Consequently, even when regulatory officials are eager to obtain the input of public interest groups, the lack of technical expertise in these groups hampers their effective participation in the rule-making process. As one regulator observed (Miles and Bhambri, 1983: 64-65), "We have solicited comments from consumer representatives. It's unfortunate, but frankly their comments are not as helpful as the ones we receive from the industry representatives because the consumer representatives don't have the resources to thoroughly analyze something of this nature."

If the historical tendency has been for the regulated groups to dominate the rule-making process through greater motivation, resources, and technical expertise, how can we account for pro-regulation groups' success during the 1970s in getting regulations which were strongly opposed by industry groups? One of the most important factors was the development of a base of political organizations, "public interest groups," which provided a vehicle for effective participation in the rule-making process. The membership of these organizations expanded greatly during the 1970s. "Between 1970 and 1971, membership in the five largest environmental organizations increased by 400,000, a 33 percent increase in one year" (Vogel, 1981: 170). In addition, during the Carter administration from 1977 through 1980, a large number of public interest advocates were appointed to key regulatory positions within the federal government.

The expanded participation of the public in regulatory politics is partly attributable to the emotional nature of the regulatory issues of the time. Environmental catastrophes, like the Santa Barbara oil spill and the Love Canal hazardous waste site, raised the consciousness of the public and motivated many previously inactive citizens to participate in public interest organizations and lobbying efforts.[3] Calamities such as these are given a good deal of attention by the press, which often serves as a catalyst motivating public participation.

Some critics of the regulatory policies of the 1970s have claimed that media sensationalism and public emotionalism clouded the issues, leading public interest advocates and regulatory officials to pursue excessive regulations ignoring the costs of the regulations they created. There is no denying that television pictures of drowning waterfowl on California beaches and toxic poisonings of schoolchildren at Love Canal and similar catastrophes create a more emotional reaction than revelations of insider stock trading. Nonetheless, pro-regulation activists have maintained that the "emotionalism" connected with these catastrophes have not clouded the issue, but rather have led to the justifiable expression of moral outrage toward corporate irresponsibility and government ineffectiveness.

Whether or not the policies which resulted during the 1970s were excessive or not is a matter of judgment. What is clear, however, is that the regulatory system is sensitive to the demands of vocal and organized groups. During the 1970s, changes in the political landscape temporarily resulted in the ascendance of pro-regulation voices. In most cases, however, the demands of the regulated industry are heard the loudest.

The Structure of Rules

Through the rule-making process, regulatory agencies seek to make explicit the requirements of the law—to specify what is fair, efficient, safe, and healthful. Depending on how the rules are drafted, enforcement officials will face different problems, requiring the use of judgment and discretion. This section examines various characteristics of the rules themselves and how these affect the enforcement process.

Regulations and criminal laws are similar in that they are both legal rules which attempt, through the threat of penalties, to influence behavior. Yet there are a number of ways in which the legal and moral characteristics of regulations differ substantially from most conventional criminal laws, such as those proscribing murder, assault, or theft.

While the violation of regulations often holds consequences as serious as the violation of criminal laws, regulations in general differ in two principal respects. First, while most conventional criminal laws relate to some specific harm that is proscribed, regulations typically relate only to the risk of harm. Second, most conventional criminal laws require some degree of culpability: intent, knowledge, recklessness, or negligence, while regulations often impose strict liability.

Conventional criminal laws make it illegal to hurt people physically and to take other people's property. For the crimes of murder, assault, robbery, burglary, theft, and arson the harm is a direct and necessary result of the crime. Regulations are not so straightforward. Many times regulations attempt to prevent harms by prohibiting the behaviors which create a *risk* that harm will occur. In this respect, regulations may be compared to drunk-driving laws. Driving while intoxicated is not inherently harmful. But driving while under the influence of alcohol or drugs does create a risk that the driver will lose control of the car and that someone will be hurt.

In a similar manner, many regulations prohibit risky behavior rather than inherently harmful behavior. For example, coal mine regulations prohibit the operation of a coal mine when methane gas reaches certain concentrations because of the risk of an explosion. When methane gas exceeds regulatory limits, an explosion will actually occur in only a small number of cases, but often enough to substantiate the riskiness of operating a coal mine under those conditions.

This characteristic of regulations holds a number of consequences, both in terms of the causes of regulatory violations and the actions of enforcement officials. In many cases, when risks are created, it is not the violator who is at risk of being injured, but third parties—consumers, workers, or the public at large. In fact, the corporation is in a position to benefit by violating regulations, thereby avoiding the costs of complying with the regulations. The violator may rationalize that probably no one will actually get hurt, and even if luck runs out and somebody does get hurt, it will be somebody else!

Since regulations relate primarily to risk-taking rather than to inherently bad or immoral behavior, violators may rationalize that "we didn't mean to hurt anybody" (Frank, 1985). This lack of evil motives has often been viewed as a reason for treating regulatory violators more leniently than conventional criminals. Thus, enforcement officials frequently are observed avoiding the imposition of penalties and relying on informal negotiations with violators to persuade them to stop violating the regulations. "No harm done" is a common justification for avoiding the imposition of penalties for regulatory violations.

A second characteristic of regulations is the lack of any requirement of culpability. The vast majority of regulations impose strict liability. That is, legal action against a violator may be undertaken even though the violation was committed unintentionally. Even if the violator took extraordinary precautions to avoid violating the regulation, the law makes violators legally responsible and subject to penalties.

Strict liability has become a part of regulations since the late nineteenth century. The reason for imposing strict liability is that, quite simply, without it the laws would be virtually unenforceable (Frank, 1986). If regulatory officials needed to prove that a corporation intended to violate a particular regulation, or was negligent in maintaining compliance with a regulation, it would be almost impossible to impose penalties under many circumstances. Decision-making and responsibility is so diffused within corporations, and so hidden from outside view, that regulatory officials could not establish that there was culpability.[4]

This characteristic of regulations also influences their enforcement. Often, enforcement officials seek to enforce regulations only when culpability can be inferred from a long history of non-compliance. Continued violation of the same rule may be assumed to be intentional, unless the violator is able to point to some extenuating circumstance.

Another characteristic of regulations concerns the specificity of the rules. One of the purposes of establishing a system of administrative rule-making is to allow the creation of more specific rules than would be possible if rule-making was left up to the legislative branch. Nonetheless, even administrative rules vary greatly in the degree of specificity they provide.

One of the principal differences between rules relates to whether they are performance standards or specification standards (U.S. Congress, 1974). A performance standard merely identifies the level of performance that an operation must attain, but does not specify how that level is to be attained. For example, in occupational health regulation, a performance standard might set a limit on the amount of lead that may be in a worker's blood. If workers in a plant showed lead levels above the standard, the plant would be in violation. The regulation would not specify any particular precautions which employers must take to prevent worker exposure to lead in the workplace. Employers could choose from a variety of potentially effective options, including both personal protective equipment and engineering controls.

Performance standards are more broad and flexible than specification standards, which explicitly specify the means to be used to accomplish a given result. Rather than identifying an objective, such as blood lead levels, the rule would specify the precise methods that must be used to protect workers from lead exposure. For example, a specification standard might require that particular types of equipment be used in plants with high concentrations of lead.

For industry, the reliance on specification standards has been cited as one of the main problems with regulation, leading to stagnation of innovation and excessive compliance costs. Industry argues that specification standards are too inflexible and lead to "site-level unreasonableness" when enforced consistently, without taking the particular circumstances of the site into account (Bardach and Kagan, 1982). Because of this site-level unreasonableness, companies are forced to comply with regulations that may be useless or even counter-productive under their own particular circumstances.

Moreover, specification standards have been blamed for reducing the level of industrial innovation. Performance standards, it is argued, create incentives for companies to find the most efficient means of meeting regulatory objectives. In the long run, this incentive for innovation may lead to the discovery of new technology that allows regulatory standards to be surpassed at lower cost. Specification standards, in contrast, lock industry into one set of technology and offer no incentives for research and innovation.

In spite of these objections to specification standards, regulatory agencies frequently rely on them because they reduce enforcement officials' need to use judgment in investigating for violations and can reduce the costs of investigation. For example, in the example above of lead in the workplace, the ease with which an investigator could determine that specific safety equipment is being used is probably much greater compared to the effort needed to obtain blood samples from workers and have these analyzed for lead concentrations.

Even performance standards may vary considerably, some being relatively vague while others are quite precise. For instance, a regulation might include the rather vague requirement that food processing areas have adequate lighting. "Adequate" is a vague term that leaves it up to the judgment of enforcement officials whether a certain amount of light is adequate or inadequate. In contrast, a more specific performance standard might require that illumination of 12 foot-candles be provided at work surfaces. This performance standard offers a precise criterion for deciding whether or not there is "adequate" light, while still allowing regulated firms to decide for themselves how to meet the standard. Both of these standards are in contrast to a specification standard which might require that a 100 watt bulb be installed every five feet.

The more vague the rule, the more enforcement officials are forced to use judgment in deciding whether the observed conditions violate regulatory standards. The more specific a rule, the more it risks being overbroad and resulting in more cost to comply than the requirement is worth. Where regulations are overly vague, enforcement officials have no choice but to exercise discretion in deciding whether or not a violation exists (Diver, 1980: 284). At the same time, however, such rules may encourage enforcement officials to construe regulatory requirements leniently. Enforcement officials err on the side of not finding a violation unless it is absolutely clearcut. On the other hand, when regulations are very specific, enforcement officials do not need to use discretion, but their failure to do so may result in unfair and illogical enforcement, which may lead to resentment on the part of industry.

Conclusion

The way in which regulatory rules are drafted influences the type of discretion demanded of regulatory enforcement officials. Dealing with risk rather than actual harm, imposing strict liability, setting performance or specification standards—all of these characteristics of regulatory rules play a role in shaping the actions of enforcement officials, to which we turn in the next few chapters.

Chapter Four will look at the investigatory process, with a particular focus on the special investigative powers available to regulatory officials. Chapter Five will then go on to pursue issues of discretion as they relate to the enforcement process.

Notes

[1] For a more detailed discussion of the legal theories and cases relating to the delegation of power to regulatory agencies, see Heffron and McFeeley, 1983: 31-39.

[2] These generalizations relate specifically to federal regulation and federal constitutional interpretations. In a number of states, the doctrine of non-delegability continues to place limits on the powers of state legislatures to rely on regulatory agencies for rule-making.

[3] The Santa Barbara oil spill has been cited as the catalyst which led to the growth of the environmental movement. On January 28, 1969 an off-shore drilling site owned jointly by Union Oil Company, Mobil, Texaco, and Gulf, located in the Santa Barbara channel, went out of control. The drilling crew's attempt to avert an explosion created geological pressures which caused a rupture in the ocean floor, spewing tens of thousands of barrels of oil into the channel. The ecological effects were devastating. Thousands of birds were saturated with oil and sunk, unable to swim; thousands more were sent to bird-cleaning stations, where many more died. The total effects on the marine ecology of the area have never been reliably estimated (Sethi, 1982).

Nonetheless, the long-term political impact of the spill is widely recognized. Immediately after the spill, Congress held hearings, the media focused on environmental issues, and a new decade of conservation and protection of wildlife began.

The Love Canal hazardous waste dump site of the Hooker Chemical Company galvanized public attention in 1979. Beginning in the 1930s or 1940s, Hooker Chemical had buried barrels of toxic wastes, including dioxin, in a meadow near Niagara Falls, New York. Decades later, after the land had been sold and a subdivision built on the site, residents began to notice strange-looking and noxious-smelling substances oozing from the ground and, in some cases, into their basements. Residents also noticed inexplicable health problems, including miscarriages and a high rate of cancer. By 1976, the New York State Department of Environmental Conservation had become aware that there were dangerous compounds in the sump pump of at least one home in the area (Brown, 1980: 15). In 1978, the state announced that it would conduct a health study, and subsequently declared an official health emergency, eventually leading to a massive evacuation and clean-up effort (Brown, 1980).

[4] In some cases, it is possible to "pierce the corporate veil" of secrecy and obtain evidence of culpability, and even criminal convictions for culpable violations. See Hochstedler (1984) for a discussion of legal theories relating to corporate criminal responsibility.

References

Administrative Procedures Act (1946) P.L. 404, 60 Stat. 237.

Bardach, Eugene and Robert A. Kagan (1982) *Going by the Book: The Problem of Regulatory Unreasonableness.* Philadelphia: Temple University Press.

Behrman, Bradley (1980) "Civil Aeronautics Board." In James Q. Wilson (ed.) *The Politics of Regulation.* New York: Basic Books.

Breyer, Stephen (1982) *Regulation and its Reform.* Cambridge, MA: Harvard University Press.

Brown, Michael H. (1980) *Laying Waste: The Poisoning of America by Toxic Chemicals.* New York: Pantheon.

Clinard, Marshall B. and Peter C. Yeager (1980) *Corporate Crime.* New York: The Free Press.

Diver, Colin S. (1980) "A Theory of Regulatory Enforcement." *Public Policy* 28: 257-299.

Epstein, Samuel S. (1979) *The Politics of Cancer.* Garden City, NY: Anchor Press.

Frank, Nancy (1985) *Crimes Against Health and Safety.* Albany, NY: Harrow and Heston.

_____(1986) *From Criminal Law to Regulation: A Historical Analysis of Health and Safety Law.* New York: Garland.

Heffron, Florence with Neil McFeeley (1983) *The Administrative Regulatory Process.* New York: Longman.

Hochstedler, Ellen (1984) *Corporations as Criminals.* Beverly Hills: Sage Publications.

Miles, Robert H. and Arvind Bhambri (1983) *The Regulatory Executives.* Beverly Hills: Sage Publications.

Pertschuk, Michael (1982) *Revolt Against Regulation: The Rise and Pause of the Consumer Movement.* Los Angeles: University of California Press.

Sethi, S. Prakash (1982) "The Santa Barbara Oil Spill." In M. David Ermann and Richard J. Lundman (eds.) *Corporate and Governmental De-*

viance: Problems of Organizational Behavior and Contemporary Society, 2nd ed. New York: Oxford University Press.

U.S. Congress (1974) *Study on Federal Regulation, Vol. VI, Framework for Regulation.* Senate Committee on Governmental Affairs, 95th Cong., 2d Sess.

U.S. v. Grimaud (1911) 220 US 506.

Vogel, David (1981) "The 'New' Social Regulation in Historical and Comparative Perspective." In Thomas K. McGraw (ed.) *Regulation in Perspective: Historical Essays.* Cambridge, MA: Harvard University Press.

CHAPTER 4

The Investigatory Process

Rules are created by regulatory agencies to clarify for corporations the limits on corporate conduct. Although many corporations can be trusted to obey the rules simply because they are the law, other corporations are tempted to violate the rules, particularly if it is cheaper or more profitable for them to break the rules than to obey them. For this reason, it is necessary to enforce the rules in order to deter corporate illegality. The first step in the enforcement process is investigation, or the discovery of illegality.

Regulatory agencies employ a variety of techniques for discovering violations of regulations. Most agencies employ some mix of reactive and proactive strategies. Reactive investigation relies on third parties, such as members of the public, to provide information relating to potential violations. After receiving this information, the agency conducts a follow-up investigation to determine whether a violation actually exists and to collect information documenting the violation for possible legal action to gain compliance. In proactive investigation, the agency goes out looking for violations, usually through the inspection of premises and the examination of records and documents.

Which of these strategies is employed, or what mix of these strategies, depends on a number of factors. In general, the more visible the violations, the more the agency is liable to rely on a reactive strategy. In water pollution enforcement, for example, complaints from the public usually pertain to conspicuous and more obvious violations (Hawkins, 1984: 376). Many housing code enforcement agencies rely on complaints from tenants and neighbors to alert the agency to code violations (Hawkins and Thomas, 1984: 12). Since many such violations are apparent to tenants, the agency investigates these violations by following up on complaints rather than by conducting routine inspections of rental properties.

Another factor leading to the choice of a reactive rather than a proactive strategy relates to the resources of the agency. In general, proactive investigation will require more resources than a reactive strategy. Thus, an underfunded agency may not have sufficient resources to mount a program of routine surveillance and inspection and may rely instead on following up on the complaints that it receives.

One disadvantage of relying on a reactive strategy is that the violations which may be most apparent to the public may not be the most serious (Diver, 1980: 276). For example, tenants may not have the expertise to discover electrical violations, which are likely to cause fire or electrocution hazards that are more serious than the cosmetic violations which tenants are apt to report. In addition, some regulatory agencies consider third party complaints to be unreliable. Housing code inspectors find that tenants make complaints as retaliation against the landlord for raising the rent or some other dispute (Nivola, 1978). Job safety inspectors suspect that workers make complaints against their employers for similar reasons (Ashford, 1976). Because of the limitations of reactive investigation, many agencies rely heavily on proactive investigative techniques for discovering violations.

Regardless of the strategy employed, the investigatory process consists of several phases. First, investigation is oriented toward the discovery of violations and the determination that a violation does, in fact, exist. Second, investigation is oriented toward collecting sufficient evidence to document the violation in case legal action is needed. Throughout these two phases, yet a third objective is sought—compliance. The process of gaining compliance is treated separately in Chapter Five.

Investigating Economic Regulatory Violations

Most investigation related to economic regulations involves the review of vast quantities of documentary evidence and the auditing of records. The first step is to study data about an industry or the behavior of particular firms in an industry to determine whether there might be illegal activities. In other words, the first step is to find a case.

Suzanne Weaver (1980: 136) describes the investigative activities of the Antitrust Division of the Department of Justice.

> The attorneys sift through several sources of information from day to day for hints of possible violations. They get complaints from citizens and consumers, from businessmen (or their lawyers) upset about competitors' practices, from congressmen helping out constituents, and from other governmental agencies. They receive reports of merger activity from documents that corporations are legally required to file. The attorneys also follow the business press and have contacts of their own.

In other agencies, the search for cases may be more focused because of reporting requirements which produce a set of data which is periodically reviewed to find evidence of regulatory violations. For example, corporations issuing shares of stock must file extensive information statements and periodic financial reports with the SEC (Bardach and Kagan, 1982: 244). Other agencies rely primarily on complaints from aggrieved customers or competitors.

In at least one agency, the decision about whether to take a reactive or a proactive investigative approach became a major policy issue. At the FTC, the commission debated whether to rely primarily on the mailbag for discovering violations (reactive) or whether it should "assume the initiative and use its scarce resources selectively to attack abuses in those sectors of the economy that most affect the consumer" (Katzman, 1980: 163). Proponents of the "mailbag" approach claimed that its major advantage is that such cases generally are related to conduct which is easier to prosecute than complex cases related to the structure of specific industries. Advocates of the proactive approach believe the reactive strategy for finding cases is wasteful because "mailbag" cases are less harmful to consumers than market imperfections which lead to anti-competitive behavior. Thus, supporters of the proactive strategy advocate greater use of industry-wide investigations and economic surveys for discovering concentrated industries that are symptoms of monopoly and oligopoly.

As this example from the FTC illustrates, the type of investigative strategy that is pursued may greatly affect the types of cases that are found. The choice of strategies is one means of directing enforcement resources from some kinds of behavior to others.

Yet, the choice of strategies is based only partially on the objective characteristics of the regulations which must be enforced. For example, Katzman found that FTC attorneys, who are convinced that gaining trial experience is the best means of advancing their own careers, preferred a reactive investigatory strategy because these mailbag cases would be less complex than the "big" structural cases which could take years to come to trial (Katzman, 1980: 164). Economists working for the same agency, on the other hand, preferred the proactive approach, which reflected their own interest in "structural cases."

The investigation of violations of economic regulations is notoriously expensive and time-consuming. For example, Katzman (1980) describes the investigation of complex structural cases at the FTC.

> The more complex cases—particularly the mammoth structural matters and industry-wide investigations—may present the attorney with great difficulties. He must devote much of his time to gathering data on concentration ratios, profitability, barriers to entry, the structure of the industry and business practices—in

short, on all key areas involved in antitrust prosecutions. Such information is not always readily available; it may take months or even years of dedicated inquiry. Attorneys may make use of a variety of techniques to obtain information: for example, subpoenas, investigational hearings (at which company officials may be called to testify), and questionnaires.

Nor is the expense and time required to investigate violations absorbed exclusively by the agency. A corporation which comes under investigation by the FTC, SEC, or another economic regulatory agency may be required to engage in expensive searches for information or documents demanded by the agency. In regulatory justice, as in criminal justice, it is often true that "the process is the punishment" (Feeley, 1979).

Investigating for Violations of Social Regulations

Like economic regulation, investigations related to social regulation may be either reactive or proactive. Water pollution officials, for example, may conduct surveys of water quality in a watershed at periodic intervals, or on the basis of a complaint from local fishermen. Nonetheless, a common technique of investigation of social regulation is highly proactive: the routine inspection. Most agencies rely on some mix of these two strategies. Whether the agency relies more heavily on one than on the other is likely to depend on the agency's goals, the nature of the violations, the number and quality of complaints coming to the agency from outside sources, and other factors.

Keith Hawkins (1984) describes the relationship between reactive and proactive investigation in water pollution enforcement in Great Britain. The proactive investigation activities of pollution control officials in Britain involve two monitoring techniques: regular scheduled sampling of rivers and major effluents and physical inspection of waterways. Sampling is conducted according to a schedule, with more important waterways or those likely to present problems being sampled more frequently than smaller rivers and streams. Physical inspection is less strictly controlled, but no less organized. Officers go where they expect to find trouble (Hawkins, 1984: 378).

Inspectors refer...to expectations generated by the polluter's occupation, demeanor during encounters in the past or behavior which mean "you generally know where to look for trouble." "If you've got a company that consistently, since you can remember, has turned out a good quality of effluent," said a supervisor, "obviously you do look at them from time to time. But you're wasting your time looking at them when [a firm you know to be bad] up the road might be doing something terrible."

Officers have less control over complaint cases; they must take complaints as they come. Complaints also demand greater attention from pollution officers. Since complaints usually relate to publicly apparent instances of pollution, the complainant may be persistent, demanding that "something be done" about the pollution which has been reported. At the same time, however, officers view complaints as "untrustworthy sources of information: untrained eyes are prone to inaccuracy and many succumb to the temptation of exaggeration" (Hawkins, 1984: 379). Nonetheless, all complaints must be taken seriously because of their potential to create a scandal, which might cause trouble for the agency (Kemp, 1984). "The involvement of a complainant can make an incident a public matter in which concern about the efficiency and responsiveness of the authority may be raised" (Hawkins, 1984: 380).

This fact results in two significant consequences. First, complaint cases take priority over proactively discovered cases. "Indeed, for many staff the working definition of a 'serious' pollution is 'basically anything that's going to cause a great amount of public reaction'" (Hawkins, 1984: 380). Second, the concern with maintaining the public image of the agency creates a desire to prevent instances of pollution from becoming apparent to the public.

According to Hawkins (1984: 381-382), "field staff make special efforts to encourage dischargers to always get in touch with them when they have any pollution control problems at all," thereby hoping to catch the pollution before it becomes apparent enough to be noticed by the public. This creates the necessity of maintaining friendly working relationships with dischargers. Officers maintain these relationships by showing "understanding" of problems and by making dischargers feel that they can trust officers. "In practical terms this means that pollution voluntarily reported will not normally be penalized" (Hawkins, 1984: 382). These observations raise an important issue: the importance of maintaining the cooperation of the firms being investigated.

Maintaining Cooperation

In regulatory investigation, the necessity of maintaining cooperation has been given a good deal of attention. Regulatory agencies are dependent on the regulated industry for information which can be crucial to attaining regulatory goals. Because of this dependence, the agency seeks to maintain the cooperation of regulated firms. If cooperative relationships can be maintained, it is argued, more and better quality information can be obtained, at lower cost to the agency, than if the agency is forced to use the legal powers at its disposal to compel information from an uncooperative subject.

This view is argued most vigorously by Bardach and Kagan. They contend that much of the information needed by regulatory agencies to discover violations of the law are possessed only by the regulated firm. Bardach and Kagan (1982: 110-111) offer the following example.

> Nursing homes, in order to receive their Medicare reimbursements, must comply with a detailed set of record-keeping and reporting regulations. The requirements are so complex that many homes hire outside "record consultants" to advise them about compliance; typically, the consultant gives the facility detailed reports on deficiencies in their present system, how records should be kept in the future, and the like.

> In California, with its legalistic enforcement system, state inspectors issue first-instance citations for violations of record-keeping rules. Moreover, according to one nursing home administrator, "The surveyor comes in and requests the *consulting report* and then writes citations for violations indicated in the consulting report....Now facilities are conducting record consultations *verbally*. They put only bland written reports in the files and say that the place is doing a terrific job and doesn't need to improve on anything, but in reality the verbal report might mention a couple of dozen areas which need improvement."

Bardach and Kagan conclude that strict, legalistic enforcement has cut off a variety of sources of information that could potentially improve compliance with regulations. They cite the reluctance of trade associations to undertake research relating to regulatory compliance as well as the more general reluctance of regulated firms to share information with the regulatory agency for fear that the information provided will be used to impose more stringent regulatory requirements or to require costly abatement of conditions.

The preferred alternative, Bardach and Kagan argue, is to use forebearance and reciprocity to gain the cooperation of regulated firms in providing necessary information. Agencies must earn the trust of regulated firms, which are assured that information that is provided will not be taken out of context or used to impose formal penalties. Regulatory officials can achieve this only by foregoing the enforcement of regulations.

In addition, the regulated industry's control over information creates a source of power which can be used to influence and control the regulatory agency. As Mitnick (1980: 211) points out, "Through control of information, the industry can succeed in coopting the regulators...making the regulators perceive the regulatory task through an informational framework and orientation provided by the industry." In short, the price of information obtained through the maintenance of cooperation may be cooptation and reduced effectiveness.

The regulatory official's ability to trade forebearance for information stems, in the first instance, from the regulated firm's belief that the agency will use its formal powers of coercion if the firm does not cooperate. If, through cooptation and bargaining, the industry is successful in reducing the agency's use of formal sanctions, the agency's power to maintain cooperation in the future may be undermined. As Bardach and Kagan (1982: 131) note, the regulatory official

> gains a hearing by virtue of his power to cause trouble for the regulated enterprise—by issuing citations, threatening legal penalties, and creating the risk of adverse publicity. "We get to see the manager right away now," said a Cal-OSHA enforcement official who had also served as an inspector in the pre-OSHA "no sanction" days.

The increased use of legal action increased the power of the inspector, giving him something to trade for the firm's cooperation, which is not available when an agency shows lenience even to non-cooperative firms.

Dealing with Ambiguity

In both economic and social regulation, the process of discovering a violation is rarely as simple as holding a yardstick up to a railing to measure whether the railing is high enough. Frequently, the inspector must exercise judgment and interpret the regulations in light of the specific circumstances which are found through the investigation. Thus, discovering violations involves more than just uncovering facts; it also requires that the investigator determine the meaning of those facts. This is particularly likely to be the case when the regulations of the agency set broad performance standards. In Hawkins' (1984: 385-386) research on enforcement activities of British pollution officers, the legal rules proscribed discharges of:

> any "poisonous, noxious, or polluting matter"....What is re-
> garded as "polluting matter" is settled by reference to the stan-
> dards in the consent to discharge the effluent [which are the
> equivalent of regulatory rules.] These mark out the parameters
> of pollution (the substances proscribed in excess) and their lim-
> its (the point at which a concentration of the substance becomes
> legally "polluting").

Sampling and laboratory analysis provide the best evidence, and the legally mandatory evidence, that illegal pollution exists. Even with this relatively precise and technical definition of pollution, however, difficulties arise. Laboratory analysis cannot always provide a reliable answer because of the potential for error in both analysis and measurement. Sometimes scientific tests do not exist which are sensitive enough to detect or measure proscribed pollution.

In addition, officers rely a great deal on their experience and intuitive knowledge of effluents to guide their investigative activities. Because laboratory resources are limited, officers rely on skill at examining effluents and water samples to determine whether there is good cause to be suspicious. Because officers are aware of the technical limitations of laboratory analysis, they are wary of results that do not match their own common-sense expectations.

Hawkins found that water pollution officers in Britain were liable to treat marginal cases with greater leniency, at least in part because of the unreliability of laboratory tests, which made the definition of violations somewhat ambiguous. "Where the precise evidence of rule-breaking is open to question, the 'deviant' is often given the benefit of the doubt" (Hawkins, 1984: 388). We found a similar relationship between ambiguity and leniency in our research of food inspection and public health enforcement. Those types of violations that could be most precisely defined, and where reliable laboratory tests existed to document a violation, were more likely to receive formal action than violations based on an inspector's judgment of whether a food operation was dirty or insanitary (Frank and Lombness, 1987).[1]

This is not always the case, however. Some agencies use vague rules as an opportunity for stretching the boundaries of their authority. For example, the Securities and Exchange Commission operates under a vague congressional mandate and a broad regulatory definition of "insider trading" (Williams, 1986: 36).

> The rules are sufficiently broad that the SEC can brand almost
> any transaction it deems unfair to be illegal insider trading. As

a result, the commission is constantly amending the rules as it goes along, sometimes defining a new kind of insider trading *after* it brings a case.

Whether an agency responds to the vagueness of rules by backing away from investigation and enforcement of marginal cases or by treating marginal cases as an opportunity to expand the reach of the law probably depends on the political environment in which the agency operates. The SEC has long been cited as a strict agency, possibly because it serves a powerful constituency of major stock traders who face serious economic losses when some of their colleagues refuse to play by the rules (Freedman, 1978: 97-100). Other agencies, however, are caught in a constant public relations campaign directed toward the regulated industry, trying to convince the industry that the agency is not seriously threatening except to the few egregious offenders.

Dealing with Limited Resources

Few public agencies complain of having too much money and too many employees. Regulatory agencies are no exception. Lack of resources is a frequently cited cause of regulatory ineffectiveness. Regulatory administrators complain that they have too few investigators to analyze the reams of data that hold clues of regulatory violations or to inspect the thousands of establishments under their jurisdiction.

Although there are isolated historical examples of dramatic shifts in the funding of regulatory agencies (see, for example, Litan and Nordhaus, 1983; Tolchin and Tolchin, 1983), there is little reason to expect the resource problems of regulatory agencies to be remedied. Consequently, regulatory agencies need to find ways of using their limited resources in the most efficient ways.

One of the suggestions for improving regulatory efficiency in discovering violations is targeted investigation. Many regulatory agencies pursue a policy of routine, periodic investigation of all regulated firms. This is most typical of agencies regulating health and safety, which commonly adopt a policy that all regulated establishments must be inspected once a year or twice a year, or at some other regular interval.[2] This policy rests largely an a deterrent rationale. It assumes that all firms are, more or less, equally likely to violate the law unless they have reason to fear that they will be caught and penalized.

The policy of routine periodic inspections is quite expensive and time-consuming, however, and diverts scarce resources to the inspection of relatively "good apples" while the violations of the "bad apple" down the road may go uncorrected because the agency lacks the resources to pursue legal action. Moreover, to the extent that a large number of regulated firms really are "good apples," the assumptions of the deterrence rationale may be incorrect.

Targeted investigation relies on a different set of assumptions. It assumes that most regulated firms will comply with regulatory requirements simply because it is the law. Only a few "bad apples" need to be deterred through the threat of legal sanctions. Therefore, regulatory agencies should target their investigative resources on those few "bad apples" (Scholz, 1984a).

The criteria that are used for deciding how to target investigative resources is crucial to the success of this policy. Some agencies leave it up to the discretion of the investigative officers, as is the case for pollution officers in Britain (Hawkins, 1984). Other agencies establish rigid criteria for determining when an on-site inspection is warranted, and investigative officers are constrained from following hunches unless these criteria are met. In these cases, serious violations may be overlooked if the criteria for triggering an inspection are unreliable.

OSHA administrator Thorne Auchter sought to adjust to budget cuts during the early 1980s by adopting a targeted investigation policy. Under this new policy, an inspector was not authorized to conduct an on-site inspection of a workplace unless the company's own accident and illness records indicated that there was a safety or health problem in the plant. If company records indicated an injury rate below the national average, no inspection of the workplace would be conducted. The stated purpose of the policy was to focus inspection resources on worksites where workers were most likely to be hurt (Claybrook, 1984: 101).

At least two things interfered with the reliability of this criterion, however. First, there is no guarantee of the truthfulness of company records. Indeed, employers have a good deal of incentive to falsify these records. Not only would a bad record trigger an inspection, but a bad accident or illness record could also result in higher workers' compensation insurance premiums. During congressional debates on the Occupational Safety and Health Act during the late 1960s, workers testified that their employers routinely "fudged" the data to improve their accident records.

Another limitation of the OSHA criterion is that it is not very sensitive to occupational diseases and other occupational hazards, such as excessive noise in the workplace. It is widely accepted that the major occupational safety and health problem in recent decades has been the proliferation of chemicals in the workplace which have chronic and latent effects. A worker exposed to benzene in the workplace today may not show symptoms for ten or twenty years. Workers exposed to chemicals, radiation, and noise in the workplace are likely to keep working steadily, until they finally fall ill. The accident and illness reports of the company will not indicate that anything is wrong. But under OSHA's criterion for on-site inspections, establishments with serious contamination problems might well escape discovery. Indeed, OSHA's policy may preclude discovery.

Just such a case occurred in Illinois in 1985. An OSHA inspector had checked the accident records of the Film Recovery Systems plant and found the company's records to be satisfactory. Unknown to the inspector, who never visited the plant but only the company offices next door, workers were being exposed to high concentrations of cyanide and were frequently leaving the work floor to recover or go home. The situation did not come to light until one worker died of cyanide poisoning (see Frank, 1985: 21-25).

This tragic example should not be read as a condemnation of all targeted investigation, but it does highlight the necessity of selecting criteria carefully. Some combination of periodic inspection and targeted investigations may well be the most effective policy. In searching for ways of improving the efficiency of investigation, regulatory policy-makers must be aware of the assumptions upon which their policies are based.

Special Investigative Powers of Regulatory Agencies

In the examples of regulatory investigations described in the sections above, a variety of investigative techniques have been mentioned, including subpoenas, interrogation of regulated persons, and inspections of records and regulated establishments. As students of the criminal justice system are well aware, police investigative activities are circumscribed by constitutional requirements of fairness and due process, particularly in regard to Fourth and Fifth Amendment rights. Protecting the rights of suspects is costly in efficiency terms. It takes more time and energy to catch a thief by following the rules of procedure than it does if one ignores or relaxes these rules.

The same holds true for regulatory investigations. Early in the history of regulation, investigation of regulatory violations was hampered by procedural requirements, based on constitutional protections. These requirements made it very difficult for regulatory officials to discover and prosecute violations of regulatory laws. Advocates of strong regulation complained that these procedures were too inefficient, and pressed for the relaxation of constitutional procedures in relation to regulatory investigation. Beginning in the 1940s, the courts entered an era of permissiveness, in which the need for efficient enforcement was held to outweigh the regulated firms' interest in privacy and due process (Heffron and McFeeley, 1983).

Novel investigatory powers have been asserted by statute and regulation and subsequently upheld by the courts as permissible for the investigation of regulatory offenses. A variety of regulatory statutes have legislated powers to regulatory agencies that allow agency officials to enter and inspect establishments and records, without probable cause that a crime has occurred. Other statutes have required regulated firms to submit various forms of evidence to the regulatory agency. This evidence, in turn, is used to determine whether the firm has violated a regulation. In some cases, laws have even required that firms come forward and admit to regulatory violations, and if they fail to do so, penalties may be invoked.

Regulated firms have not always submitted to these procedures without a fight. Businesses subject to these investigatory powers have argued that these practices violate the Fourth and Fifth Amendments to the Constitution. Although the courts were initially sympathetic to the complaints of regulated firms that these procedures were unconstitutional, beginning in the 1940s, the Supreme Court began to find the relaxation of constitutional mandates permissible in the context of regulatory investigations.

There are three kinds of investigatory tools that arguably infringe on constitutional rights: reporting requirements, mandatory submission of records and documents, and access to records and facilities for routine inspection.

The Fifth Amendment and Reporting Requirements

The Supreme Court has held that corporations have no privilege against self-incrimination (see *George Campbell Painting Corp. v. Reid*, 392 U.S. 286). As long as the criminal charges are brought against the corporation, rather than against individuals, the Fifth Amendment does not apply. A corporation cannot testify, and the Fifth Amendment cannot be used to shield corporate officials from testifying against the corporation.

There are some cases, however, where an individual may have a regulatory duty to report a violation but where that same individual may subsequently be subject to penalties. Some regulatory statutes require that certain violations be reported to regulatory officials as soon as the violation becomes known to responsible agents of the business. Often, these requirements are backed up by either civil or criminal sanctions which penalize those who fail or refuse to report known violations. In addition, penalties may also be imposed for the violation which was reported.

Some critics have commented that these reporting requirements create a classic Catch-22. If the violator reports the violation, as required by law, he or she may be penalized for that violation. On the other hand, if the violator fails to report the violation, he or she may suffer penalties for the failure to report.

In these cases, the courts have held that the central issue is whether the penalties for the violation are civil or criminal. If the penalty is criminal, the self-incrimination clause prevents the government from compelling a violator to report the violation. But if the penalties are civil, no such protection is afforded the violator.

An example of such a law is found in Section 11 of the Water Quality Improvement Act of 1970. Subsection 1161(b)(4) provides that:

> Any person in charge of a vessel or of an off-shore facility shall, as soon as he has knowledge of any discharge of oil from such a vessel or facility in violation of paragraph (2) of this subsection, immediately notify the appropriate agency of the United States Government of such discharge. Any such person who fails to notify immediately such agency of such discharge shall, upon conviction, be fined not more than $10,000, or imprisoned for not more than one year, or both. Notification received pursuant to this paragraph or information obtained by the exploitation of such notification shall not be used against any such person in any criminal case, except a prosecution for perjury or for giving a false statement.

By providing that information obtained through this mandatory reporting provision not be used in any criminal case against the person reporting the violation, Congress attempted to avoid any Fifth Amendment issues. If the statute prevented the information reported by a violator to be used in a criminal prosecution, the reporting requirement could not result in self-incrimination.

The issue was not so easily settled, however, because of the possibility of civil penalties following mandatory reporting of an oil spill. Congress gave the regulatory agency a choice of whether to use criminal or civil penalties for violations of the oil pollution act. The availability of these civil penalties ultimately led to a number of court cases in which managers that had reported violations under the reporting requirement of Subsection 1161(b)(4) were subsequently assessed civil penalties for the very violations which they had reported. These businesses asserted that the assessment of civil penalties violated the Fifth Amendment right against self-incrimination. The case of *United States v. L.O. Ward Oil and Gas Operations* is illustrative.

United States v. Ward

In March of 1975, oil escaped from an oil retention pit at a drilling facility leased by the L.O. Ward Oil and Gas Operations. A little over a week later, Ward notified the regional office of the Environmental Protection Agency that a discharge of oil had taken place. A subsequent written report of the discharge submitted by Ward was forwarded to the Coast Guard, which was the agency responsible for enforcing the oil pollution law. Based on the information it received from Ward, the Coast Guard elected to assess a $500 civil penalty against Ward.

Ward claimed that this penalty violated his Fifth Amendment right against compulsory self-incrimination and filed suit in federal district court seeking to prevent the Coast Guard and the EPA from collecting the penalty. The district court rejected Ward's arguments, although it did reduce the penalty to $250.

Ward was dissatisfied with this result and took the case on to the Court of Appeals. The Court of Appeals agreed with Ward, finding that although the penalty was formally designated "civil" by Congress, it was so punitive in nature that the Fifth Amendment rights usually afforded only to criminal defendants should apply equally to the civil penalty to which Ward was subjected after reporting the illegal oil spill. On a subsequent appeal, the U.S. Supreme Court reversed the holding of the Court of Appeals. In order to gain a richer understanding of the issues presented by this case, let us take a closer look at the decisions of both the Court of Appeals and the Supreme Court and the reasoning used by each to support its conclusions.

As noted by the Supreme Court, the "distinction between a civil and a criminal penalty is of some constitutional import. The Self-Incrimination Clause of the Fifth Amendment, for example, is expressly limited to 'any criminal case'" (U.S. v. Ward, 1980: 248). Normally, the question of whether a statute is civil or criminal is decided on the basis of a statute's construction. First, the court must consider whether Congress explicitly or implicitly indicated a preference for one label or the other. Second, even where Congress has indicated that the penalty is to be civil, the courts may reject that characterization if the statutory scheme is "so punitive either in purpose or effect to negate" the civil designation (U.S. v. Ward, 1980: 249). In other words, even if Congress explicitly labeled a statute "civil," if the penalty is quite punitive, the courts should treat the statute as criminal with respect to the provision of constitutional rights.

With respect to the penalties for oil pollution, Congress could not have made its intentions more explicit. In 1899, the Rivers and Harbors Act provided criminal penalties for discharges of oil into navigable waters. Over seventy years later, in 1970, Congress again addressed the problem of oil pollution, retaining the criminal provision of the 1899 act and adding a new civil penalty provision.

But the second question, regarding the punitive nature of this civil penalty, proved to be contentious. The Court of Appeals, in considering Ward's case, found that the civil penalty was, in fact, punitive in nature. The Court of Appeals based its conclusion on an analysis of the civil penalty in relation to seven considerations previously set forth by the Supreme Court for deciding these sorts of questions (see *Kennedy v. Mendoza-Martinez*, 372 U.S. 144).

The Supreme Court disagreed with the characterization of the civil penalty as really criminal in nature, although the court only briefly discussed its analysis of the penalty in light of the *Mendoza-Martinez* criteria. In holding the civil penalty to be civil for purposes of the self-incrimination clause, the Court put considerable weight on the supposed purpose of the civil penalty. If only a retributive or deterrent purpose could be found, the Court indicated that it might agree with Ward that the penalty should be considered criminal in nature, at least with respect to the self-incrimination clause. But, in this case, the Court found that the penalty was more like civil damages than it was like punishment for a crime. The Court implied that the civil penalty might be a compensation for the damages sustained by society or for the cost of enforcing the law.

The major issue presented by the court decisions in the *Ward* case relates to the ambiguities and inconsistencies in the use of the words *criminal* and *civil* in designating penalties. This is a highly salient issue given the historical trend toward greater and greater use of civil rather than criminal penalties for regulatory violations (Frank, 1986). Although the Supreme Court has provided some standards for holding a "civil" penalty to be criminal in nature for the purpose of applying constitutional protections, the *Ward* decision indicates that the Court prefers these standards to be very narrowly interpreted. Unless there are strong reasons for treating the penalty as criminal, a "civil" designation by Congress will normally be sufficient to exempt the proceedings from those constitutional protections relating only to "criminal cases."

The problem with this interpretation, of course, is that civil penalties are a relatively recent invention of Congress, applying to behavior that at other times, or under other circumstances, may be dealt with criminally. Moreover, civil fines are often at least as painful as criminal fines, but defendants are not afforded similar protections.

Another Fifth Amendment issue is raised by laws requiring that regulated firms keep records of their activities. These records are then required to be made available to regulatory officials in investigating whether firms have violated regulations. For example, nursing homes are required to keep records on patient care and staffing. These records can be useful in calling potential violations to the attention of investigators and providing information supporting legal action against the violator.

Nonetheless, the practice certainly raises Fifth Amendment issues, particularly in those cases where criminal penalties are available as an enforcement option. As one Supreme Court Justice has remarked, "It would no doubt simplify enforcement of all criminal laws if each citizen were required to keep a diary that would show where he was at all times, whom he was with and what he was up to" (quoted in Heffron and McFeeley, 1983: 193). Obviously such a practice would be roundly condemned as an infringement of constitutional rights. Yet the Supreme Court has held that in relation to regulatory matters, such a requirement is not impermissible (Heffron and McFeeley, 1983: 194).

Mandatory Submission of Records

Another area of controversy relates to the subpoena of records to be used in investigating a regulatory violation. Early in the history of regulation, the courts had held that a subpoena for records could be issued only upon probable cause. It restrained agencies from going on "fishing expeditions," whether these general investigations were for the purpose of rulemaking or enforcement (Heffron and McFeeley, 1983: 184). Later, however, the courts became more permissive.

In *U.S. v. Morton Salt* (1949) the Supreme Court held that regulatory agencies may order the production of reports and records as long as this authority has been granted to the agency, the order is not vague, and the reports and records ordered are reasonably relevant to matters under the jurisdiction of the agency. A *subpoena duces tecum*, or subpoena of records, may be issued without any probable cause determination. The agency does not need to show evidence that a law has been violated or that it is likely that a search of the records will produce evidence of illegality. As long as the order is lawfully ordered, reasonably specific, and relevant, it will be upheld by the courts. The primary reason given for dispensing with probable cause is that there is no violation of privacy—no government official demanding entry.

Firms subject to subpoena argue, however, that the demand for records can be oppressive in scope, even if not a violation of privacy (*Hermann v. CAB*, 1956). For example, when the Justice Department filed an antitrust suit against American Telephone and Telegraph during the 1970s, the company estimated that records demanded by the government (Weidenbaum, 1977: 147):

could cost $300 million and 20,000 man-years of effort, including a search of seven billion pages of material. One Justice Department request from AT&T included every piece of paper "prepared, sent, or received since January 1, 1930, which relate or refer in whole or in part to, or which constitute instructions, directives, or suggestions regarding the purchase by AT&T or any Bell company of telecommunications equipment from Western Electric.

Such intrusive and burdensome regulatory demands may be made without any showing of probable cause.

Search and Seizure and the Administrative Inspection

In some cases, rather than issuing a subpoena for records or documents, an agency may have statutory authority to enter a regulated establishment and demand the opportunity to examine books and records. A common variation of this authority is the power of regulatory investigators to enter and inspect regulated premises to search for evidence of violations. These grants of authority have raised questions concerning traditional search and seizure law as developed by the courts under the Fourth Amendment to the Constitution.

The Fourth Amendment protects citizens from "unreasonable" searches and seizures. The precise meaning of what is "unreasonable" has evolved through almost 200 years of judicial interpretation. The courts have found a basic right to privacy underlying the Fourth Amendment and have held that that right to privacy may be infringed by the government only if it has a very good reason for doing so.

In general, the "good reason" put forth by the government in the investigation of conventional crimes is that the government has "probable cause" to believe that evidence of a crime will be discovered if the government is given the opportunity to search. There is also a presumption that, unless "exigent" or special circumstances exist, the search should be conducted only after the government has obtained a search warrant from a judge. The warrant requirement is designed to place a check on enforcement authorities by providing a neutral determination of whether there is, in fact, "probable cause."

The Supreme Court, over the years, has created a number of exceptions to both the warrant requirement and the requirement of probable cause. For example, if police are in "hot pursuit" or if evidence of a crime is in "plain view," the police need not take time out to obtain a search warrant but may go ahead and conduct the search immediately on the basis of probable cause. In some cases, even the requirement of probable cause has been relaxed. In *Terry v. Ohio*, the Supreme Court held that the police may conduct a pat-down search of a detainee's outer clothing to locate weapons which might be used by the detainee to injure the officer or bystanders. Customs officials and immigration officials have also been granted exceptions to the usual probable cause requirement.

Regulatory inspections of records and premises have been held to be yet another exception to the probable cause requirement. Like the other exceptions noted above, the Court has attempted to justify this exception as reasonable by balancing the practical needs of the enforcement agency against the limited privacy interests being violated by the search.

Frank v. Maryland

The first major decision of the Supreme Court on this issue came in 1959 in the case of *Frank v. Maryland*. The case involved the attempt of a local health inspector to search through Frank's house in search of rats or evidence of rats. The inspector, acting on the complaint of a neighbor, inspected the exterior of the house and found evidence of rodent infestation. The inspector asked Frank for permission to inspect the basement of the house, but Frank refused. The next day, the inspector returned with two police officers but, knocking on the door, received no answer. The inspector then proceeded to swear out an arrest warrant, not a search warrant, on the basis of Frank's alleged violation of a Baltimore ordinance which prohibited an owner or occupier from refusing or delaying an inspection whenever there was suspicion of a nuisance. The penalty was a forfeiture of twenty dollars. Frank was arrested, found guilty, and fined twenty dollars. Frank appealed the conviction, eventually taking his case to the Supreme Court.

In deciding the case, the Court took the familiar balancing approach. It found the privacy interests at stake to be minimal. It noted that the inspection was attempted at a reasonable time; there was no "midnight knock on the door." Nor was forced entry attempted over the objections of the owner (*Frank v. Maryland*, 1959: 882).

> Thus, not only does the inspection touch at most upon the periphery of the important interests safeguarded by the Fourteenth Amendment's protection against official intrusion, but it is hedged about with safeguards designed to make the least possible demand on the individual occupant, and to cause only the slightest restriction on his claims to privacy.

Against this slight violation of privacy the Court balanced the community's need to protect the general welfare. The Court placed substantial emphasis on the historic use of such inspections, noting that thousands and thousands of inspections had been made under the Baltimore ordinance for more than a century and a half. In particular, the Court found that this history had taught, first, that the power to inspect dwellings was indispensable for the maintenance of community health and, second, that the experience of those many years had not yet revealed any abuse of the power.

Balancing the limited invasion of privacy against the long practice of such inspections and the necessities of public health, the Court upheld Frank's conviction for refusing the inspection. Not all of the justices agreed however. The dissent of Justice Douglas foreshadowed future court decisions on this issue. Justice Douglas viewed the Court's ruling as an abrogation of the Fourth Amendment. He urged that a warrant should be required, but interestingly, raised the possibility that the "probable cause" showing required to obtain the warrant might be different from what is required in a criminal case.

Camara v. Municipal Court of San Francisco

The majority in *Frank v. Maryland* held that a regulatory search was reasonable, without a warrant and without probable cause, and that refusal to allow the inspection could be punished by a fine. This holding was reversed by the Supreme Court in 1967, when the Court took a position similar to that advocated by Justice Douglas in his dissent in *Frank*.

In *Camara*, as in *Frank*, the case involved the inspection of a home. In this case, the inspection was requested by San Francisco building inspectors doing routine inspections for violations of the housing code. As in the *Frank* case, the inspector had evidence to suspect a violation, this time based on information from the building manager. When the inspector demanded the opportunity to inspect the dwelling, the occupant, Camara, refused because the inspector lacked a warrant. On two subsequent occasions, Camara refused again, leading to the filing of a criminal complaint against Camara for refusing to permit a lawful inspection. Camara appealed to the Supreme Court. The Supreme Court overturned its decision in *Frank v. Maryland* and held that the Fourth and Fourteenth Amendments provide household dwellers the right to demand that regulatory officials obtain a warrant before they demand entry to inspect.

The Court found that "except in certain carefully defined classes of cases, a search of private property without proper consent is unreasonable unless it has been authorized by a valid search warrant" (*Camara v. Munici-*

pal Court, 1967: 935). It noted that the *Frank* decision had been widely interpreted as carving out an exception to the warrant requirement, and went on to re-examine the arguments of the *Frank* majority.

The Court in *Camara* rejected the contention of the majority in *Frank* that the interests at stake in regulatory inspections were "merely peripheral." The Court found it anomalous to interpret the Fourth Amendment as protecting privacy only when the individual is suspected of criminal behavior. In addition, the Court noted that oftentimes the violations toward which the inspection was addressed were actually crimes after all, carrying criminal penalties.

The Court also believed that the *Frank* decision underestimated the purposes and advantages of requiring a warrant (*Camara v. Municipal Court*, 1967: 937).

> Under the present system, when the inspector demands entry, the occupant has no way of knowing whether enforcement of the municipal code involved requires inspection of his premises, no way of knowing the lawful limits of the inspector's power to search, and no way of knowing whether the inspector himself is acting under proper authorization. These are questions which may be reviewed by a neutral magistrate without any reassessment of the basic agency decision to canvass an area.

Finally, the Court found that the public interest in regulatory enforcement offered no justification for dispensing with the warrant requirement. "The question is not, at this stage at least, whether these inspections may be made, but whether they may be made without a warrant" (*Camara v. Municipal Court*, 1967: 938).

The Court disagreed, however, with *Camara*'s contention that the warrant should be issued only upon a showing of probable cause that a particular dwelling contains violations. The Court then went on to use the same balancing argument relied upon by the Court in *Frank*. This time, however, rather than using this argument to permit a warrantless inspection, the Court used the balancing test to justify a probable cause determination different from that used in criminal cases. According to the Court, "In determining whether a particular inspection is reasonable—and thus in determining whether there is probable cause to issue a warrant for that inspection—the need for the inspection must be weighed in terms of the reasonable goals of code enforcement" (*Camara v. Municipal Court*, 1967: 939).

Unlike a search warrant, obtaining the warrant described here would not require a showing of evidence that a law has been violated and that evidence of the violation can be found at the place designated to be searched.

Instead, regulatory officials are required only to justify the inspection of a particular place in terms of the goals of enforcement and the overall inspection program. This is an easy standard to meet, especially since many of the enabling statutes of regulatory agencies specifically indicate that some form of routine inspection is anticipated.

The *Camara* decision was upheld more recently in relation to the Occupational Safety and Health Act. In the *Marshall v. Barlow's* decision (436 US 307, 1978), the Court once again upheld the *Camara* warrant requirement. In this case, however, three justices issued a vigorous dissent to the opinion, taking issue with the majority's relaxation of the probable cause requirement for regulatory warrants. In particular, these justices viewed the regulatory warrant authorized by the majority as a category of "general warrants" like those which the framers of the Constitution sought to prevent. They viewed the warrant as an unnecessary formality as well, adding little to the information and protections already afforded by statute. In other words, the dissenting justices advocated a return to the *Frank v. Maryland* doctrine that warrantless inspections were reasonable under the Constitution.

None of the decisions or dissenting opinions have ever contended that regulatory inspections ought to meet the same warrant and probable cause standards as searches conducted in the course of a criminal investigation. The Court has consistently found that the public's interest in preventing dangerous conditions outweighs the limited privacy interests of those subject to regulatory inspections.

It is true that the Court has used the potential for danger in other contexts to find a limited invasion of privacy to be reasonable under the Fourth Amendment. For example, the Court held that the police officer's interest in protecting himself from harm in a street confrontation with a suspect justified a limited pat-down of the suspect's outer clothing (*Terry v. Ohio*). Similarly, danger was at least one of the justifications for allowing an immediate search of an arrestee's clothing (*Chimel v. California*). Danger was also one of the reasons cited by the Court in *Opperman v. South Dakota* justifying police search and inventory of impounded vehicles. In each of these cases, as in the regulatory context, the Court justified what it found to be a limited invasion of privacy on the basis of the need to prevent potential danger.

The Court has not been consistent in its application of this justification, however. Rather than limiting its holding to those inspections that are concerned with dangerous or unsafe conditions, the Court has implied that the relaxed standards for regulatory inspections apply to all such inspections, even if these are merely concerned with protecting property interests, such as preventing "unsightly conditions [which] adversely affect the economic values of neighboring structures" (*Camara v. Municipal Court*, 1967: 939).

The Court has implied that even in the absence of any danger, a regulatory inspection without probable cause is permissible because of the limited privacy interests that are at stake. Authorities do not agree, however, that businesses have only a limited privacy interest. Regulated businesses have attempted to underscore their need for privacy, pointing to the maintenance of "trade secrets" as one of the principal reasons for seeking to limit government access to information. This concern has been heightened in recent years with the passage of open records laws and the Freedom of Information Act. Bardach and Kagan (1982: 110) observe that, under these laws, "inspection reports in agency files are public records, and they commonly are obtained by manufacturers seeking information about their competitors' failings and capabilities." These are legitimate interests in privacy which are independent of a firm's interest in concealing evidence of wrongdoing. Although the Supreme Court has held that these privacy interests are minimal, none of the opinions specifically analyze what these interests are.

Perhaps the ultimate justification for the relaxed standards for regulatory inspections rests on the third factor the Court has weighed in its balancing test: the historical acceptance of routine regulatory inspections. Regulatory inspections have been conducted, with infrequent objection, since the late nineteenth century. The Court appears to have taken the position that since it had gone on so long without any observable harm being suffered by those subject to these searches, there is little reason to stop them entirely. Those justices who have supported the warrant requirement have done so in an attempt to remove the possibility of the abuse of these powers, by giving the person whose privacy is to be violated the opportunity to demand that a neutral magistrate determine that the inspection is legally authorized and reasonable within the goals of the regulatory program.

To make any more drastic change simply has appeared out of the question. It is not that holding regulatory officials to the same standards as police would make regulatory enforcement impossible, but that it did not appear unreasonable to allow regulatory officials to go on inspecting as they had for decades.

Given the widespread reliance on routine inspection and examination of records in regulatory enforcement, and relatively widespread acceptance of these practices among the regulated public, it is hard to envision any change toward a more restrictive interpretation of the Fourth Amendment in the future. The result is somewhat inelegant and inconsistent with Fourth Amendment principles as these are applied in other areas of law enforcement, but, for now, this is the law.

The Services of an Expert

Our discussion up to now of the investigatory process has proceeded from the perspective that investigation is the first step toward enforcement action against a violator. In many cases, however, regulatory action is completed at the investigatory stage. This may happen when no violations are discovered, when the violator immediately corrects any violations that are found, or when the investigator uses his discretion by deciding that formal action is not required under the circumstances. Chapter Five will go on to explore this third possibility in greater detail. To conclude this chapter, however, let us look at the investigatory process as a service.

In Chapter Two, we noted that regulatory agencies serve both control and service functions. The investigation process offers one of the opportunities for even the most control-oriented agencies to offer service to regulated firms. Investigation by the regulatory agency serves as a double check on the firm's own compliance and surveillance system. Investigation also involves a large measure of education to the regulated industry. The inspector takes a consultant role, pointing out violations and potential problems to the firm, explaining the significance of violations, and showing the firm how to correct the violation in a cost-effective manner.

In those instances in which the firm is motivated to comply with the regulations, the inspector provides a "second pair of eyes," recognizing problems that even the most conscientious firm may have inadvertently overlooked. The regulated firm and the regulatory agency have complementary competences. "Corporate experts will know of problems undetected by regulatory inspectors unfamiliar with specific plants and overly focused on enforceable violations, but inspectors will see other potential problems overlooked or neglected by experts too busy in planning new projects or too timid to challenge operating personnel" (Scholz, 1984b: 150). Recognizing their own shortcomings, some regulated firms may welcome regulatory oversight. This is regulation as service.

Unfortunately, some agencies fail to capitalize on this opportunity to build trust and communication with regulated firms. Many agencies do not seem to be cognizant of the importance of expertise. They hire inspectors who are not really qualified for the job and provide minimal training, frequently amounting to little more than handing an inspector a rule book and an inspection sheet, and sending the novice inspector out to do the job.

If inspectors lack sufficient technical expertise, they are likely to be of little service to the firms they inspect. Without adequate skills, the inspector will not know where to look for evidence of violations and will not know how to correct the violations that are discovered. Without a high degree of expertise, the inspector may even be a detriment to the firm and to regulatory compliance. Inspectors who lack expertise are sometimes more likely to "go by the book" when they are unsure of their judgment. They are not capable of assessing a firm's novel solution to a compliance problem or of appreciating special circumstances that make literal compliance with the regulations counter-productive or unreasonable. Moreover, regulatory inspectors with inadequate expertise quickly lose the respect of regulated firms, making them less willing to accept the inspector's judgment without question. Ultimately, lack of training can erode respect for the agency in particular and for government in general.

Many agencies feel compelled to demonstrate their efficiency by maintaining high numbers of inspections. Because of limited resources, this goal frequently can be achieved only if inspectors spend as little time as possible on each inspection. Consequently, some agencies discourage inspectors from spending time talking to managers about compliance problems. This time is looked at as unproductive time because it cannot be expressed in quantitative terms, i.e., numbers of inspections, number of samples taken, number of violations discovered (see Diver, 1980: 277).

In addition, even those agencies that recognize the consultant role that inspectors can play do little to augment this role. Bardach and Kagan (1982: 145) note that agencies "could enhance inspectors' ability to play this role if they consciously tried to serve as a data bank of abatement techniques...." Instead, most inspectors must rely on their own creativity, based on their expertise, as well as compliance tips that they come across through their contacts with many different firms.

Although service cannot be substituted for deterrence and control, especially since not all violators are motivated to comply with the law, it can make regulatory agencies more effective and efficient, provided that inspectors are knowledgeable, that they are given the time and the incentive to act as consultants, and that consultation does not come to be substituted for legal action when the violator proves to be uncooperative. The enforcement and consultant roles are really complementary. As we shall argue in Chapter Five, ideal enforcement requires the appropriate mix of both these strategies.

Conclusion

Regulatory investigation relies heavily on the voluntary cooperation of regulated persons and firms in providing information and access to facilities for discovery of violations. Maintaining the continued cooperation of regulated firms appears to depend upon the agency's ability to communicate the reasonableness of its intentions. Agencies frequently exchange both information and a degree of leniency for the cooperation of the regulated firm in providing information as well as complying with regulations.

When the regulated are uncooperative, the power of regulatory agencies to compel information and access has been widely upheld by the courts. Regulated persons or firms may be criminally penalized for failure to deliver records that have been requested or for refusing to allow inspection of regulated premises. While the rationale for allowing such broad authority may be questioned, there is little chance that these powers will be significantly diminished as regulation becomes a more and more important and pervasive presence in modern life.

Notes

[1] This result may be due, in some cases, to the inexperience and lack of legal expertise of regulatory officials responsible for deciding whether to pursue legal action. For example, in an agency in which officials are poorly trained and, hence, "incompetent" to make judgments regarding the legal sufficiency of evidence, officials may forego legal action except in those instances where the evidence is "cut and dried." Thus, although court action may be successful if based solely on the regulatory official's expert judgment that conditions violate the law, such cases may be avoided because the official doubts his own judgment and is unaware that his judgment may be sufficient in a court of law.

This raises some interesting problems in regard to the captured agency; see Chapter Six. If all enforcement decisions are made by upper-level administrators, but these administrators lack the same expertise as inspectors, industry may be able to exploit the relative incompetence of administrators, convincing them that the evidence is too subjective to stand up in court.

[2] For example, in public health enforcement, statutes require periodic inspections in an effort to provide the minimum level of effective surveillance. Inspections are designed to be preventive and to provide a service, as well as to discover existing violations. More frequent inspection obviously increases the cost of inspection, but it may be more effective if inspectors are able to catch situations before they become problems.

References

Ashford, Nicholas A. (1976) *Crisis in the Workplace.* Cambridge, MA: MIT Press.

Bardach, Eugene and Robert A. Kagan (1982) *Going by the Book: The Problem of Regulatory Unreasonableness.* Philadelphia: Temple University Press.

Camara v. Municipal Court (1967) 387 US 523.

Claybrook, Joan (1984) *Retreat from Safety: Reagan's Attack on America's Health.* New York: Pantheon.

Diver, Colin S. (1980) "A Theory of Regulatory Enforcement." *Public Policy* 28: 257-299.

Feeley, Malcolm (1979) *The Process is the Punishment.* New York: Russell Sage Foundation.

Frank, Nancy (1985) *Crimes Against Health and Safety.* Albany, NY: Harrow and Heston.

_____ (1986) *From Criminal Law to Regulation: A Historical Analysis of Health and Safety Law.* New York: Garland.

Frank, Nancy and Michael J. Lombness (1987) "Using Judgment: Inspectors' Perceptions of the Seriousness of Violations," *Journal of Crime and Justice* (forthcoming).

Frank v. Maryland (1959) 359 US 360.

Freedman, James O. (1978) *Crisis and Legitimacy.* New York: Cambridge University Press.

Hawkins, Keith (1984) "Creating Cases in a Regulatory Agency." *Urban Life* 12: 371-395.

Hawkins, Keith and John M. Thomas (1984) "The Enforcement Process in Regulatory Bureaucracies." In Keith Hawkins and John M. Thomas (eds.) *Enforcing Regulation.* Boston: Kluwer-Nijhoff.

Heffron, Florence with Neil McFeeley (1983) *The Administrative Regulatory Process*. New York: Longman.

Hermann v. CAB (1956) 237 F2d 359.

Katzman, Robert (1980) "Federal Trade Commission." In James Q. Wilson (ed.) *The Politics of Regulation*. New York: Basic Books.

Kemp, Kathleen (1984) "Accidents, Scandals, and Political Support for Regulatory Agencies." *Journal of Politics* 46: 401-427.

Litan, Robert E. and William D. Nordhaus (1983) *Reforming Federal Regulation*. New Haven: Yale University Press.

Mitnick, Barry M. (1980) *The Political Economy of Regulation*. New York: Columbia University Press.

Nivola, Pietro S. (1978) "Distributing a Municipal Service: A Case Study of Housing Inspection." *Journal of Politics* 40: 59-81.

Scholz, John (1984a) "Cooperation, Deterrence, and the Ecology of Regulatory Enforcement." *Law and Society Review* 18: 179-224.

_____ (1984b) "Reliability, Responsiveness, and Regulatory Policy." *Public Administration Review* 44: 145-153.

Tolchin, Susan and Martin Tolchin (1983) *Dismantling America: The Rush to Deregulate*. Boston: Houghton Mifflin.

U.S. v. Morton Salt (1950) 338 US 632.

U.S. v. Ward (1980) 448 US 242.

Weaver, Suzanne (1980) "Antitrust Division of the Department of Justice." In James Q. Wilson (ed.) *The Politics of Regulation*. New York: Basic Books.

Weidenbaum, Murray L. (1977) *Business, Government, and the Public*. Englewood Cliffs, NJ: Prentice-Hall.

Williams, Monci Jo (1986) "What's Legal—And What's Not." *Fortune* 114: 36-37.

CHAPTER 5

Enforcing Regulations

After a violation has been discovered, regulatory officials must decide what to do about it. This decision has two facets: (1) whether to seek full compliance at all and (2) how to persuade or compel the violator to comply. The decision that is made with respect to each of these questions is only partly determined by the nature of the violation. A number of other factors press on agency officials to influence their enforcement decisions.

Research on regulatory enforcement has attempted to delineate types of regulatory agencies, distinguishing between agencies that adopt a "compliance strategy" and those that rely on a "deterrence strategy." A compliance strategy "is primarily concerned with preventing violations and remedying underlying problems," a deterrence system "with detecting offenses and punishing violators" (Hawkins and Thomas, 1984: 13). Each of these types of strategies has been identified with patterns of discretion. In a compliance strategy, following the letter of the law is less important than achieving the goals which the regulation was designed to reach. In addition, a compliance strategy relies more on negotiating with violators than on the use of legal action to gain compliance. The legal powers of inspectors are used, if at all, only as a threat, to remind the violator that "there is an easy way and a hard way" of getting compliance (Frank and Lombness, 1987). The threat of legal action is just one of a range of compliance tools used by the inspector, which includes rewards, a friendly relationship, and providing information and expertise.

"In a deterrence system, on the other hand, the enforcement style tends to be accusatory and adversarial, leading to routine reliance on formal processes" (Hawkins and Thomas, 1984: 13). A deterrence strategy tolerates less discretion in the identification of violations; inspectors "go strictly by the book" (Bardach and Kagan. 1982). Inspectors settle for nothing less than full compliance with regulations, refusing to overlook seemingly minor, even trivial violations and being unwilling to listen to the excuses of violators, even when they have valid justifications under the circumstances.

Kagan and Scholz (1983) suggest that the theories regulators have about why violations occur influence which of these two contrasting styles of enforcement action they will use. According to Kagan and Scholz, inspectors hold three major theories. One theory is that the violator is an "amoral calculator" who will violate regulations anytime the benefits to the violator of non-compliance exceed the costs of punishment. A second theory holds that the violator did not intend to violate the law, but failed to develop an organizational structure capable of implementing an effective compliance system. Lack of skill and lack of attention are the primary culprits under this theory. Finally, some violations occur through the regulatory equivalent of civil disobedience, when the violator disregards the law in principled disrespect for what the violator views as a foolish or unjust law.

Problems arise in regulatory enforcement when enforcement officials assume that all violators fit a single theory of causation rather than recognizing differences between good apples, bad apples and marginal firms. Kagan and Scholz suggest that enforcement officials need to respond flexibly, depending on the causes of non-compliance. If a violator has compliance problems because he is organizationally incompetent, ideal enforcement calls for consultation with the violator to assist him in establishing an effective compliance system. If a violator is a political citizen resisting an unfair law, persuasion is the best response. If there are good reasons for the regulation, these should be communicated. If there are no good reasons, then the rule should be changed or an exception granted; in other words, the regulatory agency should be responsive to "political citizens." Finally, if the violation occurs through an amoral calculation of the profitability of violating the law, the response should be the prompt imposition of sanctions to deter future violation.

These different responses imply different tools which regulatory officials must use to gain compliance. Some of these tools are primarily legal remedies and sanctions for deterring violations or controlling violators. Others depend more on the skill and perseverence of regulatory officials in their attempts to persuade firms to comply with the law.

Tools for Deterring Violations

Regardless of whether an agency is oriented primarily toward a compliance or a deterrence approach, from time to time legal action will be the only means available for gaining compliance and achieving the goals of regulatory officials. Regulatory law offers a wide range of penalties and remedies for attaining compliance. Not all agencies possess all of the options noted here, but most agencies are able to choose among several different legal strategies for gaining compliance. Some of these are administratively-imposed, which means that the agency may impose the penalty without having to obtain a judicial order. Administratively-imposed penalties include summary actions, which may be taken without holding a hearing prior to taking action, and a variety of other administrative options that may be ordered following an administrative hearing.   In other cases, the agency must go to court in order to have the penalty legally imposed.   Judicially-imposed sanctions include both civil remedies and criminal penalties.

Administrative Remedies and Penalties

As noted above, administrative remedies and penalties can be imposed by the regulatory agency without any court action.   In other words, regulatory officials possess the authority to penalize violations directly, rather than that authority being vested in the courts.   By giving regulatory officials the authority to impose remedies and penalties, the costs and delays of seeking court action are eliminated.   In large metropolitan areas, where both the criminal and civil courts are burdened by large case backlogs, regulatory officials may avoid legal action entirely if they need to go to court to get a penalty imposed.   Administrative imposition offers greater potential for speedy resolution of the case.

Like the rule-making process, administrative adjudication is governed by administrative law, typically an administrative procedures act, which in some cases may be modified by the enabling legislation related to a particular agency.   Early in the history of administrative regulation, administrative adjudication was informal and result-oriented with little attention paid to the formalities of the rule of law.   Over time, however, most regulatory agencies have been pressed to adopt more formal adjudicatory procedures that rely on adversarial processes and the requirements of due process. With the development of formal adjudicative processes, regulatory agencies did not abandon the more informal, result-oriented strategies, however. Instead, prior to pursuing formal adjudication an agency may engage in negotiations resulting in remedies such as a consent order or other "voluntary" agreements.

Some of the major administratively-imposed remedies and penalties are cease-and-desist orders; special, consent, and summary orders; license suspensions and revocations; and administratively-imposed fines.

Cease-and-Desist Orders

A cease-and-desist order is the administrative equivalent of a judicial injunction or restraining order.   It orders the person or corporation to halt a particular activity that the regulatory agency views as a violation of regulations.   For example, the Federal Trade Commission (FTC) possesses the authority to order advertisers to cease and desist deceptive advertising practices.   Other agencies may order companies to reduce pollution, make certain information available, modify sales policies, take affirmative action, or require other actions that will bring the corporation into compliance (Clinard and Yeager, 1980: 86). Failure to comply with a cease-and-desist order may result in the corporation being held in criminal contempt or may subject the corporation to civil fines for violating the order. Cease-and-desist orders are probably most useful where the laws defining proscribed behavior are relatively vague and unclear. The cease-and-desist order provides an opportunity for the agency to specify what the law requires in relation to the specific activities of the firm in question. In effect, the order provides more specific notice of the requirements of the law.

Special Orders

While the cease-and-desist order focuses on the future conduct of a regulated firm, special orders are oriented toward correcting past conduct. Like cease-and-desist orders, special orders are frequently used by agencies which operate under particularly broad and vague regulations.

An example of a special order is a recall notice of the Consumer Product Safety Commission. When the Commission finds that a product is unsafe, it may order the manufacturer to recall the product. The recall is particular to that product and is not based on any specific standards which the product failed to meet, but on a record of injuries related to the product.

Consent Orders

In many cases, rather than an agency taking unilateral action by issuing an order that a firm cease or desist or take some action to remedy a violation, the agency engages in negotiations with the firm, attempting to persuade the firm to take action without the agency having to pursue formal action. The Administrative Procedures Act provides for an opportunity for firms to meet with regulatory officials prior to commencement of formal action in an effort to arrive at an informal disposition (Heffron and McFeeley, 1983: 209). These negotiations take place in closed sessions, which has led some public interest groups to complain of the reliance of regulatory agencies on consent orders. For example, when the Equal Employment Opportunity Commission (EEOC) negotiated a consent order with the steel industry, requiring the industry to pay more than $30 million dollars in backpay to employees who had been discriminated against, women and minority groups complained that because they were excluded from the negotiations, the industry was able to "buy its way out" of legal troubles for a small price (Heffron and McFeeley, 1983: 210).

Clinard and Yeager (1980: 87) found that consent orders were one of the most common "sanctions" against corporations. In many cases, consent orders amount to little more than a promise not to violate the law in the future, without any admission of illegality in the past nor any remedy for violations which occurred in the past. Moreover, regulated firms will avoid immediate compliance and pursue negotiation of a consent order if they believe that this will be faster and cheaper (Langbein and Kerwin, 1985: 877). Despite these potential criticisms, however, consent orders remain popular for much the same reason that plea-bargaining remains popular in the criminal justice system. Regulatory officials argue that without consent orders, enforcement action would be impossible in many cases.

Summary Orders

A summary order is an administrative order, which may be issued without a hearing prior to the order taking effect, preventing the sale or movement of goods that are in violation of the law or to stop operations that violate the law. For example, the Wisconsin Department of Agriculture, Trade, and Consumer Protection has the authority to issue a holding order against any food that is suspected of being adulterated or misbranded and that may injure consumers. Under the holding order, the owner of the goods may not move or sell them until the holding order is lifted. The holding order provides enforcement officials with an opportunity to temporarily remove an item from commerce while laboratory and court procedures are pursued to determine whether the item violates the law.

Similarly, some state agencies that enforce work safety rules possess authority to halt operations that create a substantial risk of harm. Thus, the enforcement agency possesses the authority to suspend operations until the dangerous condition is corrected.

The individual or firm subject to the order may demand a hearing, but the hearing usually need not take place before the order takes effect. The primary justification for allowing an agency to take action prior to a hearing is to prevent danger or injury to the public. The Supreme Court has established a three-point test for determining whether summary action is justified. In determining whether summary action is necessary and appropriate, the Supreme Court directed agencies and the courts to consider (1) the government interest in efficiency and immediate action, (2) the severity of the action and the interests of the person subject to that action, and (3) the risk of erroneous action (*Mathews v. Eldridge*, 1976: 335). In effect, this three-point test suggests that summary orders are permissible whenever there is a need for immediate action, as long as the action is not too severe and the risk of error is not too high.

License Suspension or Revocation

Another sanction which is available to enforcement authorities is the suspension or revocation of a license or permit. As was discussed in Chapter Two, many activities require a license, and license requirements have been created to serve a variety of purposes.

In addition to the purposes cited earlier, licensing systems provide another means of sanctioning those who violate regulatory requirements. Regulatory agencies are given the authority to suspend or revoke the licenses of anyone who violates regulations. In some cases, enforcement officials have the authority to summarily suspend a license. In other cases, a hearing must be held prior to the suspension or revocation. In either case, suspension of a license prevents the licensee from engaging in the licensed activity until the license is reinstated, which may be a period of days or months. A revocation is a more or less permanent removal of a license. Suspension or revocation of a license can be a very severe penalty, since it may prevent a business from carrying on its normal business activities. For instance, if a restaurant has its restaurant license revoked, it may no longer operate and is effectively out of business.

Administratively-imposed Civil Fines

Some agencies have been given the authority under their enabling statutes to impose fines without having to go to court. These civil penalties are imposed administratively. The advantage of administratively-imposed fines is that it saves the regulatory agency the time and trouble of going through the court system (Goldschmid, 1973). Given the backlog under which most courts operate, it is advantageous to the agency to be able to short-circuit the court process by imposing penalties and going to court only in those cases in which the violator seeks to appeal the penalty.

Judicial Penalties and Remedies

Each of the penalties or remedies described above is available to the regulatory agency without the agency having to go to court to obtain authority to impose the penalty. These administratively-imposed penalties offer regulatory agencies greater flexibility by making it easier for the agency to impose penalties. In some cases, however, the enabling statute requires that the agency obtain court authorization for the penalties which it seeks. In these cases, the power of the regulatory agency is circumscribed by the decisions of the court.

A variety of penalties or remedies may be obtained through court action. These include injunctions, civil suits, judicially-imposed fines, and criminal sanctions.

Injunctions

An injunction serves the same general purpose as a cease-and-desist order or a holding order or similar administrative action. The purpose is to prevent a person from doing something, or continuing to do something, because it violates the law or because it is socially injurious or not in the public interest. In order to obtain an injunction, the regulatory agency must present evidence in court which demonstrates that the circumstances meet the statutorily prescribed standards for issuing an injunction. The judge then issues a court order restraining the activities which the agency alleges are in violation of regulatory standards. A temporary injunction may be issued following an *ex parte* proceeding, in which the subject of the injunction does not have a right to appear. A temporary injunction restrains the activity for only a few days. In order to obtain a temporary injunction, the regulatory agency would usually have to show some urgent reason why the activity must be halted immediately.

A permanent injunction may be issued only after a hearing in which the subject of the injunction has an opportunity to be present and to offer evidence. Violation of an injunction may result in a fine or imprisonment.

Civil Suits

Civil suits by regulatory agencies against violating firms may occur in a wide variety of circumstances. In some cases, the statute that defines the agency's powers may create a "right of action," allowing the regulatory agency to sue the violator. The object of the civil suit might be to obtain a court order that the violator follow certain procedures, or it might be an action to obtain damages in the name of the state agency. For example, the EEOC may bring suit on behalf of a victim of employment discrimination. The object of the suit might be to force an employer to hire a particular applicant or to pay damages for its illegal discrimination against an applicant. Similarly, the Justice Department may bring a suit against firms for engaging in anti-competitive practices.

Judicially-imposed Civil Fines

As noted earlier, some regulatory agencies have the authority to impose monetary fines without having to go to court. In other cases, the power to impose penalties is vested in the courts, and regulatory agencies must petition a judge to impose the penalties it seeks against a violator. Requiring that the agency go to court to have penalties imposed serves to discourage agencies from utilizing penalties because of the burdens and uncertainties of going to court. Where court action is the only remedy available, it is not unusual for regulatory agencies to conclude that it is more efficient to seek voluntary compliance from those violators who can be persuaded to comply without court action, and to forego any action against those few intransigent violators that refuse to comply without some coercion.

Criminal Action

Many of the statutes establishing regulatory authority include criminal provisions, creating criminal penalties against those who violate regulations. For example, the Occupational Safety and Health Act provides criminal penalties for any person or corporation that willfully causes the death of an employee. The Sherman Antitrust Act provides criminal penalties for restraint of trade. State laws frequently provide criminal penalties for the sale of adulterated food or drugs.

The use of criminal penalties has become controversial in recent years. Some commentators argue that equity and just deserts demand that criminal penalties be imposed for the harmful acts of corporations. Others counter these arguments with utilitarian arguments resting on the inefficiency of criminal sanctions in dealing with corporate misbehavior (see Fisse and French, 1985).

Shortcomings of Legal Sanctions

In research by Clinard and Yeager (1980) on the 500 largest industrial corporations, the most common "sanctions" were voluntary recalls and consent orders. Although these corporations committed a large number of violations, formal legal sanctions were imposed in very few cases. At least one reason for this is the perception that legal sanctions are not very effective.[1] Three problems plague most regulatory agencies in relation to legal sanctions.

First, many agencies do not possess a wide variety of legal sanctions. It is not uncommon for an agency to have very limited choices in selecting an appropriate sanction. For example, an agency may have the choice of issuing a cease-and-desist order or initiating criminal action. In many cases, both of these options may seem too heavy-handed in relation to the seriousness of the violation. Consequently, the agency is easily persuaded to avoid any formal enforcement action because the only options available are too severe.

Second, many of the sanctioning options available to regulatory agencies are not readily available because of long delays between the decision to invoke formal action and the final resolution of the case. This is particularly true for those sanctions requiring court action, but can be equally true for administrative actions if the agency lacks the resources to prepare and adjudicate the cases which are initiated. Because of the prospect of delay, regulatory officials may come to view legal action as too slow to effectively deal with regulatory problems, which are often dynamic and rapidly changing.

Third, sanctions are frequently viewed as too weak to have any effect against amoral calculators. Regulatory officials complain that such violators view administrative fines and $100 criminal fines as merely another cost of doing business. Regulatory officials frequently conclude that the effort of seeking legal action is not worth it when the penalties that can be imposed are too small to deter anyway.

Tools for Persuading Compliance

For these and other reasons, regulatory officials also rely on a number of persuasion tactics to gain compliance. These tactics attempt to change the attitudes or beliefs of violators in order to change their behavior.

Rewarding Compliance

Regulatory officials cannot offer direct monetary rewards for compliance, but they can offer reciprocity and lenience to those firms that have been generally cooperative and compliant. Through the use of lenience as a reward, an inspector attempts to build or maintain a good working relationship with a firm. Rewarding firms with lenience also creates a sense of obligation, which the inspector can call on in future interactions with the firm, especially if the firm faces a more serious violation in the future. As Bardach and Kagan (1982: 134) point out, "simply refraining from treating someone as if he were a criminal gives the inspector a reputation for reasonableness—something he can use in asking the regulated firm for significant and perhaps costly changes in procedures or facilities."

Using Friendly Relationships

Using forebearance as a reward is one means regulatory officials use to develop a friendly and cooperative relationship with managers of regulated firms. An inspector may also attempt to create a sense of identification between himself and the managers of regulated firms. By engaging in small talk, finding mutual interests, and showing understanding for the problems managers face, the inspector develops a relationship with managers in which managers see the inspector as a person rather than as a bureaucrat. If a feeling of liking and a sense of identification can be established, a violator may be willing to make some changes simply to "help out a friend." The relationship is built on mutual respect and understanding.

One of the dangers of using this tactic as a means of gaining compliance is that identification and friendship is a two-way street which the violator may use to obtain undeserved concessions from the inspector. Some regulatory agencies, wary of this danger, rotate inspector's areas frequently so that inspectors do not have an opportunity to develop close relationships with managers of firms.

Providing Information

One of the important tools regulatory officials use to gain compliance is information. Frequently, violators are unaware that what they have been doing is a violation, and even after it has been pointed out to them, they do not understand why it is a violation. Unless the inspector explains the significance of the violation and the purpose of the law, the violator is apt to presume that the violation is trivial and the law is stupid. By providing information to violators, inspectors can change these negative and resistant attitudes, and gain the cooperation and compliance of the violator. Providing information appeals to the violator's rationality, rather than demanding compliance on the basis of the inspector's legal authority alone. In essence, providing information answers the resistance epitomized by the phrase, "Why should I?"

Inspectors can also foster compliance by providing information about cost-effective methods of gaining compliance and organizational changes to prevent future violations. For example, food inspectors will suggest that food establishment operators establish a cleaning schedule that explicitly fixes accountability for the cleanliness of areas and pieces of equipment. They also provide information about cleaning techniques and cleaning products which make it easier and cheaper to maintain the establishment.

Threats and Legitimate Authority

Another common tactic of regulatory officials is to bluff: to threaten legal action, even though they have no real intention of carrying out the threat (Hawkins, 1983). In some cases, the inspector may just barely hint that he is threatening, by pointing out that "this is the law" and "you could be penalized." In other cases, inspectors may lead the violator to believe that they are preparing the case for legal action by making an elaborate show of collecting evidence and carefully documenting the violations.

Perhaps the most overt form of threat used by regulatory agencies is the warning letter. Many agencies have a policy of following up on certain kinds of violations with an "official" warning letter, informing the violator of the law, the conditions which violate the law, and the legal action that could (or will) be taken unless those conditions are corrected. Regulatory officials disagree about the effectiveness of warning letters in gaining compliance. According to some regulatory officials, violators almost always improve their compliance after receiving a warning letter. Other regulatory officials are more critical, calling warning letters "paper bullets." These critics claim that warning letters lose their effectiveness through too frequent use. Violators quickly learn whether warning letters are serious or just an idle threat that is likely to result only in another warning letter, rather than in the threatened legal action.

The Right Tool for the Job

Because of the wide range of formal and informal tools available to regulatory officials for gaining compliance, regulatory officials have the opportunity to fit the tactics they use to the specifics of a particular violation and violator. Except for those agencies that are extremely legalistic, in which every violation leads to some type of legal action, most regulatory officials initially attempt to gain compliance by using the tools of persuasion, and only when these have failed will they move on to engage in legal action against the violator. The wide range of compliance tactics available to regulatory officials promotes flexibility. Taking advantage of this flexibility is a key characteristic of ideal enforcement.

The Enforcement Ideal

In describing the "good inspector" Bardach and Kagan (1982: 150) admit that their portrait "very nearly endows him with the wisdom of Solomon, the craftiness of Ulysses, and the fortitude of Winston Churchill."

Their observation is apt, for ideal enforcement does require regulatory personnel who are highly trained, highly motivated, confident, and courageous.

Our thesis in examining the characteristics of ideal enforcement, however, is that some regulatory agencies and some regulatory environments are more (or less) conducive to ideal enforcement than others. Regulatory agencies can adopt policies which foster ideal enforcement by their staff, or which impede it. The environments in which regulatory agencies operate — the political environment in particular — can create pressures supportive of ideal enforcement or of less-than-ideal performance by the regulatory agency. To look at ideal enforcement solely in terms of the individual qualities of inspectors or agency managers would be simplistic and misleading. While top-notch personnel helps, even the best personnel cannot function effectively if at every turn they face an obstacle to using "good" discretion and flexible enforcement.

"Good" Discretion

Good discretion promotes the fairness and effectiveness of a regulatory agency. Levin (1984: 9) points out that it is impossible for a firm to meet "every limit every minute of the day. No facility can avoid occasional spills or upsets, or the 20-year veteran who turns the wrong valve and empties the tank into the river." As long as the violation is not extremely serious and normal precautions were taken against its occurrence, "good" discretion may call for overlooking such a violation. Good discretion means rewarding good apples with leniency when they have an occasional problem, which reinforces the future cooperativeness of conscientious firms.

Compensating for site-level unreasonableness is the other major situation in which discretion can be used to actually promote the goals of the agency. Site-level unreasonableness is inevitable when general rules are applied across a large number of firms (Bardach and Kagan, 1982: 25). Discretionary enforcement provides a form of individualization of the rules to the specific circumstances of the case. Put negatively, it means not being nit-picking and rigid about what constitutes compliance.

Bardach and Kagan report an example involving noise pollution and an OSHA requirement that factory noises be "engineered out" rather than requiring employees to wear "personal protective equipment," such as earplugs and earmuffs. In a particular plant, the projected cost of "engineering out" the noise was $60,000, but noise levels in the plant would still not be reduced below the required level of 90 decibels. Because of numerous uncontrollable sources of noise within the plant, workers would still have to wear earmuffs. Requiring full compliance with the letter of the law (engineering out the noise) when this is clearly infeasible, unproductive, or useless, is site-level unreasonableness. Using "good" discretion in ideal enforcement means making allowances in these sorts of situations, without compromising the level of protection or compliance "intended" under the law. This requires that regulatory officials use "good judgment."

In addition to using discretion about the level of compliance that is necessary and appropriate under given circumstances, ideal enforcement involves tailoring the response to the characteristics of the violator. Flexible enforcement takes the causes of the violation and the past performance of the violator into account. Rather than treating all violators as though they were "bad apples" undeserving of trust, only those violators who have shown themselves to be untrustworthy should be "treated like criminals." At the very least, flexible enforcement means giving people an even break.

Ideal enforcement also takes past performance into account. Those firms with a good record of compliance are given more rope and are under less intense surveillance. Good apples will be treated like good apples, with the expectation that they are doing the best job that they can and increased enforcement will only detract their attention from the job of maintaining compliance. Ideal enforcement means reciprocating for past cooperation by overlooking occasional minor lapses in compliance.

This brief sketch of ideal enforcement will no doubt become even more clear as it is contrasted with the alternatives: legalistic enforcement which takes an extreme deterrence approach and voluntary compliance which takes an extreme compliance approach. Sadly, research on regulatory enforcement suggests that the ideal is much more rare than either legalistic or voluntary compliance.

Voluntary Compliance

The predominant enforcement style of the majority of regulatory agencies—federal, state. and local—has been to exercise a great deal of discretion and to rely on voluntary compliance. Even during the decade of the 1970s, which has been excoriated as the decade of legalism, the majority of regulatory agencies, particularly the hundreds of state and local agencies, continued their traditional patterns of overlooking almost all violations, making allowances, and continually delaying compliance. If this is the predominant pattern, there must be powerful forces at work pushing regulatory agencies in this direction.

In Chapter Six we will be discussing the processes of agency capture and cooptation. These processes describe the structural and social psychological foundations for the development of voluntary compliance. Agency capture means that agency policies are dominated by the preferences of the regulated industry. While many industries may welcome a degree of government intervention, they also seek to contain government efforts within certain bounds, to assure that the costs of regulation do not spiral to levels higher than industry would be willing to pay voluntarily. Captured agencies view their role primarily in terms of service. While the specific processes of capture and cooptation are described in subsequent chapters, we will take this opportunity to describe the causes and consequences of a voluntary compliance policy.

If ideal enforcement means using "good" discretion, voluntary compliance frequently means using "bad" discretion. Inspectors allow violations to continue unabated, even when these violations are significant in terms of the goals of regulation and impact on the public. Rather than looking at the regulations as setting the floor or minimum level of acceptable behavior, regulations are viewed as the optimum, and regulatory officials allow regulated firms considerable leeway in falling below regulatory standards. For example, food regulations require that food processing areas be free of rodents because of health dangers associated with having rodents in food processing areas. An agency that pursues highly discretionary enforcement is likely to overlook rodents in food processing areas as long as droppings are not found on food contact surfaces. Inspectors in such agencies express the view that one is always going to have rodents in food operations. A rodent-free environment is looked at as a laudable goal, but not as the operating standard.

In some cases, however, firms fall so far below the "goals" of the regulations that regulatory officials can no longer overlook them entirely. Nonetheless, nothing is done to compel the violator to come into compliance. Instead, the agency relies on a range of persuasion tactics in the hope that the violator can be coaxed into voluntarily complying. Taking formal enforcement action is avoided, unless some compelling reason for taking action arises.

Voluntary compliance agencies typically engage in repeated inspections of non-compliant firms. While one purpose of these reinspections can be to establish that the violator is really doing nothing to comply and to build a case against the violator, frequent reinspection is also used as a tool to gain compliance. Inspectors have referred to this as inspectional harassment. The hope is that the violator will become so annoyed with having the inspector around all the time that he eventually makes an effort toward compliance. The violator need not come into full compliance, however. As long as the violator makes enough progress to eliminate the worst aspects of the violation, the inspector will ease off, even if the firm as a whole is still operating well below industry-wide compliance standards.

Moral suasion is also relied on to persuade the violator to comply. Although this can be an effective technique, it is likely to be ineffective with those violators who are truly amoral calculators. Without a credible threat of penalties, such violators continue to flout the law and the inspector's authority.

One of the perverse effects of voluntary compliance is that "good apples" are placed at a competitive disadvantage. Bad apple firms are allowed to cut costs by cutting corners on regulatory compliance. Since some firms are motivated to act responsibly and to comply with regulations even without the threat of penalties, these firms will continue to invest in compliance efforts. Over time, however, the pressures of the marketplace force many firms that would like to be good apples to curtail their own compliance efforts. The result is an overall reduction in the level of compliance in the regulated industry.

A second perverse effect is the impact on field enforcement personnel. Frequently these men and women enter regulatory professions because they want to help people and do something socially useful. In time, however, they are demoralized by their inability to take any effective steps against violators. A culture of non-enforcement develops, and "the practice of backing away from legal conflict can sometimes become such a habit that the inspectorate loses all thirst for aggressive enforcement, even when it is badly needed, and loses enforcement know-how" (Bardach and Kagan, 1982: 43).

In agencies that rely on voluntary compliance, inspectors frequently lack technical training as well. Poorly trained and inexperienced inspectors are primarily concerned with not making a mistake; however, that is defined by the agency. If the agency is most intolerant of those mistakes in which the inspector enforces when the agency does not want it, then lack of training will increase the degree to which inspectors avoid enforcement. Lacking confidence in their judgment, and wanting to avoid "trouble," these inspectors are likely to "err on the side of leniency in the absence of externally supplied motivation" (Diver, 1980: 285).

A third negative consequence of voluntary compliance is that enforcement action is brought against only the weakest and most inept violators, even though more powerful firms may have more significant violations (Frank and Lombness, 1987; Hawkins and Thomas, 1984). Through lack of experience, regulatory officials come to doubt their ability to successfully prosecute a case against a violator. In the few legal actions that the agency does initiate, if the violator puts up a strong and apparently competent legal fight, the agency is likely to drop its charges. In contrast, the violator who mounts an unsophisticated legal challenge offers to the agency an opportunity to establish an enforcement record, which it duly reports in its annual report and in its budget requests.

Voluntary compliance agencies are also more likely to pursue legal action only against politically weak violators. Large firms, or smaller firms that are closely connected to powerful organizations, are frightening adversaries. Whatever legal action is taken is likely to be directed against small, unrepresented firms that carry little clout with the agency.

Finally, agencies pursuing voluntary compliance create an environment in which corruption can flourish. It is common to view corruption as a *cause* of reliance on a voluntary compliance approach. According to this view, the reason that inspectors do not take more vigorous action against violators is because they are on the take. The converse can also be true, however. In agencies in which gaining compliance is no longer the goal, the taking of bribes or gifts is easily rationalized. Because the agency does not expect inspectors to maintain a high level of compliance in the firms they inspect nor to bring large numbers of legal actions, favoritism in exchange for money or favors is easily hidden from superiors. Moreover, superiors' own deference to powerful violators creates a suspicion among inspectors that superiors themselves may be accepting bribes. These suspicions can serve to fuel inspectors' own rationalizations. This is not to say that all agencies that pursue voluntary compliance are corrupt, or even that most of them are, only that the voluntary compliance strategy creates an environment conducive to corruption (see Frank, 1984).

This portrait of the voluntary compliance agency suggests that "bad" discretion is based more on the violator's capacity to create "trouble" for the agency than it is on the seriousness of the violation or the character and attitude of the violator. Legal action is taken along the course of least resistance, rather than where it is most needed. This creates a rather dismal picture of regulatory enforcement, characterized by weak-kneed and discriminatory action.

The causes of this sad state of affairs lie primarily in the political environment of regulatory agencies. When the political environment of a regulatory agency is dominated, if not monopolized, by industry groups seeking unobtrusive regulation, a voluntary compliance policy is likely to develop. If there is no organized interest group to put countervailing pressure on the agency, to press for more vigorous enforcement, industry pressures will hold sway. Regulatory officials, always concerned with avoiding "trouble," shrink from angering any firm that might be able to "rock the boat." Only if the violation is so significant that it threatens to become public, which could cause plenty of trouble, does the agency take decisive action. But even in these cases, the habit of seeking voluntary solutions can be so ingrained that effective legal action is delayed, sometimes until after it is too late.

A regulatory agency in such an environment receives no rewards or positive recognition for upholding regulatory requirements. Just the opposite, in fact, occurs; regulatory administrators receive complaints directly from businesses and from legislators that even modest efforts are "too harsh" and enforcement efforts are characterized as "Gestapo tactics." In time, agency personnel learn how to avoid these kinds of complaints. The answer is voluntary compliance.

Legalistic Enforcement

Bardach and Kagan preface their book on "regulatory unreasonableness" with the comment that legalistic enforcement is *the* problem facing contemporary regulatory agencies. While we take issue with this characterization of the main problem in modern regulatory bureaucracies, there is no question that legalistic enforcement in several important federal regulatory programs became a thorn in the side of business during the 1970s. Bardach and Kagan outline both the positive and negative consequences brought by legalistic enforcement.

On the positive side, tougher enforcement resulted in speedier compliance, greater clout for the regulatory agency with regulated firms, and changes in corporate management designed to keep companies within the law. Bardach and Kagan cite a number of examples in which legalistic enforcement appears to have made the difference between lackadaisical efforts to gain compliance and prompt compliance with regulations. Compliance specialists in corporations, whose job it is to make sure that the company is complying with regulations, have found their budgets increased and have achieved greater authority within the corporation. Compliance specialists are able to use the threat of enforcement by the legalistic regulatory agency as a lever in supporting their own requests for changes in equipment or procedures. Legalistic enforcement makes the regulations salient; they can no longer be ignored (Bardach and Kagan, 1982: 93-99).

Against the backdrop of weak enforcement that had been characteristic of most regulatory agencies up until the 1970s, these are significant accomplishments, particularly in light of the serious health problems which contemporary regulations frequently address. Nonetheless, these gains have been purchased at a cost. Bardach and Kagan note that there have been a number of perverse effects of legalism.

As a result of legalistic enforcement, inspectors "are expected to detect, document, and prosecute violations, rather than engage in an open-ended search for 'problems'" (Bardach and Kagan, 1982: 102). As a result, the attention of the inspector is narrowly focused on the rule book, causing him to overlook other potential hazards that may not yet be covered by the rule book. Bardach and Kagan note that the inspector's focus in turn influences company personnel, who respond by focusing on technical compliance rather than on the overall quality of compliance. Finally, "such diversion leads managers and compliance specialists to denigrate the inspectors, to characterize them as ignorant and legalistic nit-pickers, and to resist rather than cooperate with them" (Bardach and Kagan, 1982: 104). A retired corporate manager declared, (Clinard, 1983: 106) "Some regulations are so asinine and costly that they result in negativism toward government and thus their violation. Middle management says: 'So what the hell; they are crazy fools in the government.' There is, as a result, much discretion in middle management and top management as to whether a regulation is really important or not."

Legalism also creates resentment. The implication of legalistic enforcement is that corporate managers cannot be trusted to comply with the law. For those managers who are making good-faith efforts to comply and to do a good job, this implication is strongly resented. Fines imposed for trivial violations are doubly resented as unfair because they show an apparent disregard for the effort that the company has exerted to be compliant. The result is minimal compliance. Rather than operating in a responsible fashion and dealing with hazards, whether the rules require it or not, some managers vent their resentment by doing only as much as the regulations require, and no more.

Similarly, firms cut off cooperation with the regulatory agency. Firms become more secretive, less willing to share information about potential problems, less willing to consult with the agency and get the agency's input, because the company has no assurance that the agency will not turn around and cite the firm for a violation. All of this amounts to greater resistance, including a greater willingness to contest agency actions in administrative hearings and in courts. In part, the increase in contested cases is simply a result of the stakes being higher. But the "bad blood" that develops between the regulatory agency and industry appears to be another cause of greater resistance on the part of regulated firms.

Finally, when the resistance becomes widespread among the regulated industry, the industry moves the fight to the policy level, seeking budget cuts and legislative limits on the agency's authority. Just such a backlash by industry against the legalistic enforcement of the 1970s appears to be the major cause of the contraction of regulatory action in the 1980s (see Claybrook, 1984; Tolchin and Tolchin, 1983).

Given the perverse effects of legalistic enforcement, one wonders how such a policy could have developed in the first place. The development of legalistic enforcement in the 1970s can be traced to a number of special circumstances at the time. First, the most legalistic agencies of the period were designed to be that way, though certainly the architects of these programs were not cognizant of some of the negative side-effects they would create. Enforcement of occupational safety and health and environmental regulations had historically been weak and heavily influenced by industry. Reformers in the 1960s and early 1970s sought to replace this system with a regulatory program that would be less vulnerable to "agency capture" (Bardach and Kagan, 1982: 45; see Chapter 6 for a detailed discussion of agency capture).

> From this perspective the reform agenda was clear: (1) install new regulators, preferably at the federal level (where proregulation public interest groups could concentrate their efforts), rather than at the even more discredited state or local level; (2) write more comprehensive and explicit regulations, without gaps and "balancing" language that would permit [technical] defenses; (3) curtail administrative discretion and leniency by more specific and stringent rules and by advocacy-group participation in rule-making and enforcement; and (4) enhance deterrence by increasing the severity, speed, and consistency of sanctions.

Given the mounting political clout of the public interest groups during that time, Congress proved sympathetic to this reform agenda, and passed a number of new regulatory initiatives that incorporated many of the suggestions of the reformers. Statutes were made more stringent, requiring that particular goals be met within specified time limits. Fines were increased, and some regulatory legislation provided for mandatory fines. The law limited the discretion of inspectors to overlook violations and to postpone enforcement action. These requirements were backed up by closer scrutiny of regulatory activities and provisions allowing for citizen suits against recalcitrant agencies.

These laws emerged out of a very specific political climate, one that was characterized by conflict between powerful industry forces and a burgeoning collection of public interest groups, spearheaded by Ralph Nader. Although this was not the first time in history that proregulation groups had organized to oppose industry and demand regulation (the populist movement for antitrust and safety regulation comes to mind), these groups did possess something previous groups had not: a theory of regulatory failure. This meant that simply getting legislation passed was not enough for these reformers. They recognized that it is the *implementation* of the regulations that really counts. Being wary of the threat of regulatory capture and mistrustful of the motives of industry, they constructed a detailed reform program. More importantly, they would not go away once the law had been passed.

For the first time in history, regulatory officials found themselves serving two masters, having to be accountable to conflicting interests. Every decision of regulatory officials came under severe scrutiny. The politically safe course, under these circumstances, was to play the game strictly by the rules, to avoid making discretionary and individualized decisions that would require complex justifications. Since the new regulatory laws already provided the framework for limited use of discretion, it was relatively easy to implement such a policy.

Although a political environment characterized by conflict was perhaps the most important factor leading to legalistic enforcement, it was by no means the only one. Another important factor may well be the management dilemma posed by the rapid increase in the size of enforcement staffs. Frequently, there were not enough candidates with the necessary qualifications, so less-than-qualified candidates were hired. Nor did the agencies have time for in-depth training. With minimal qualifications and training, inspectors were not trusted by agency managers to use discretion wisely, so their discretion was strictly curtailed. Inspectors, in turn, recognizing their own limitations, were more comfortable sticking to the rule book on inspections. Lacking technical expertise and the confidence borne by training and experience, they did not trust their own judgment to make discretionary decisions in the field.[2]

Finally, it has been suggested that at least some of these perverse effects were the result of a cynical effort on the part of regulatory administrators to make the reform program fail. For example, administrators of OSHA during the Nixon administration chose to adopt, wholesale, thousands of voluntary industry standards as regulations. Many of these voluntary standards related to insignificant conditions and led to the notorious reputation of OSHA inspectors citing employers for such violations as cracked toilet seats in restrooms (Page and O'Brien, 1973). Like police officers who agitate for higher wages by strictly enforcing the law, writing tickets for every jaywalking and mile-over-the-speed-limit violation they see, some administrations may have used the tough provisions of the reform laws purposely to create a backlash.

In sum, the main factors leading to legalistic enforcement were laws which tightly circumscribed regulatory discretion, a political environment which put regulatory agencies in the middle of a pitched battle between proregulation and antiregulation groups, and the exigencies of supervising a massive new workforce of inexperienced and poorly trained inspectors.

It would be incorrect to suggest that reformers wanted regulators to become officious nit-pickers. Over time, however, the political and organizational climate fostered a culture in which such attitudes were rewarded. Or, at any rate, rewards were not forthcoming for being otherwise. The question that has yet to be answered is whether the goals of the reformers can be achieved without engendering the perverse effects of legalism. Can we achieve ideal enforcement? Before we can answer this question, we need to look in greater detail at the problems of agency capture and cooptation that legalistic enforcement was designed to avoid.

Conclusion

Regulatory agencies possess a wide range of sanctioning powers that may be used to gain compliance with regulations. Despite these sanctioning options, however, most regulatory agencies rely on voluntary compliance and informal negotiations to persuade violators to comply with regulations. Formal action is perceived by many regulatory officials as causing delays and creating excessive work for the agency. In addition, formal action increases the resistance of regulated firms, which may result in a power-play, which regulatory officials are fearful they would lose. Only during a brief period during the 1970s in certain federal agencies did agency officials rely heavily on formal sanctioning powers to deter violations and compel compliance. This shift in regulatory policy was brought about as a result of reform efforts of well-organized proregulation groups seeking to remedy the regulatory failures of the past. The reforms were effective in many ways, but ultimately created so much resentment and hostility that many of the reforms were reversed a few years later after business re-grouped to oppose the legalistic policies of the reformed agencies.

Discretion is a good and necessary part of the compliance process. But discretion can be abused. When discretion is consistently used to appease industry, the agency is captured. A captured agency no longer mediates between the interests of the public, which is to be protected through regulation, and the interests of the regulated industry. Instead, it uses its discretion to advance the goals of regulation only so far as industry interests permit. This, we contend, has been and is the dominant pattern in regulatory agencies. The next chapter explores the processes of agency capture in greater detail.

Notes

[1] In addition to the perception that legal action is not effective in deterring corporate violations, legal action may also be avoided due to industry pressure and influence. These reasons will be explored more fully in Chapter 6.

[2] It is important to note, however, that poor training contributed to legalistic enforcement only because the organizational environment was already pushing inspectors in that direction. Poorly trained and inexperienced inspectors (and managers) are primarily concerned with not making a "mistake" that will betray their ignorance and incompetence. When the type of mistake that the organization is most likely to sanction is that in which an inspector fails to take action when he or she should have under agency policy, inspectors who lack training and expertise will tend to take action in questionable cases. If there is any chance that a condition *might* be a violation, an inspector in a legalistic agency will take formal action. In a voluntary compliance agency, just the opposite is likely to occur when an inspector lacks expertise. In these agencies, the mistakes that are most likely to be organizationally sanctioned are those in which an inspector took formal action when agency policy is to use informal tools. In these agencies, lack of training is more likely to result in leniency.

References

Bardach, Eugene and Robert A. Kagan (1982) *Going by the Book: The Problem of Regulatory Unreasonableness.* Philadelphia: Temple University Press.

Claybrook, Joan (1984) *Retreat from Safety: Reagan's Attack on America's Health.* New York: Pantheon.

Clinard, Marshall B. (1984) *Corporate Ethics and Crime: The Role of Middle Management.* Beverly Hills: Sage Publications.

Clinard, Marshall B. and Peter C. Yeager (1980) *Corporate Crime.* New York: The Free Press.

Diver, Colin S. (1980) "A Theory of Regulatory Enforcement." *Public Policy* 28: 257-299.

Fisse, Brent and Peter A. French (1985) *Corrigible Criminals and Unruly Law*. San Antonio: Trinity University Press.

Frank, Nancy (1984) "Policing Corporate Crime: A Typology of Enforcement Styles." *Justice Quarterly* 1: 235-251.

Frank, Nancy and Michael J. Lombness (1987) "Using Judgment: Inspectors' Perceptions of the Seriousness of Violations." *Journal of Crime and Justice* (forthcoming).

Goldschmid, Harvey J. (1973) "An Evaluation of the Present and Potential Use of Civil Money Penalties as a Sanction by the Federal Administrative Agencies." A report in support of recommendation 72-6. Washington, D.C.: Administrative Conference of the United States.

Hawkins, Keith (1983) "Bargain and Bluff: Compliance Strategy and Deterrence in the Enforcement of Regulation." *Law and Policy Quarterly* 5: 35-73.

Hawkins, Keith and John M. Thomas (1984) "The Enforcement Process in Regulatory Bureaucracies." In *Enforcing Regulation*. Boston: Kluwer-Nihjoff.

Heffron, Florence with Neil McFeeley (1983) *The Administrative Regulatory Process*. New York: Longman.

Kagan, Robert and John Scholz (1983) "The 'Criminology' of the Corporation and Regulatory Enforcement Strategies." In Keith Hawkins and John M. Thomas (eds.) *Enforcing Regulation*. Boston: Kluwer-Nihjoff.

Langbein, Laura and Cornelius M. Kerwin (1985) "Implementation, Negotiation and Compliance in Environmental and Safety Regulation." *Journal of Politics* 47: 854-880.

Levin, Michael H. (1984) "Regulating Industry II: Securing Compliance: The Options." Paper presented before the Law and Society Association. Boston, MA.

Mathews v. Elridge (1976) 424 US 319.

Page, Joseph A. and Mary Win O'Brien (1973) *Bitter Wages*. New York: Grossman.

Tolchin, Susan and Martin Tolchin (1983) *Dismantling America: The Rush to Deregulate*. Boston: Houghton Mifflin. Boston: Houghton Mifflin.

CHAPTER 6

Agency Capture—Concept and Process

As we have seen, one of the common criticisms of the regulatory system is that far too often regulatory policies and regulatory action favor industry at the expense of the public. Independent regulatory commissions, like the ICC, CAB, FCC, and others, have been accused of granting competitive advantages to the regulated industry and shutting out non-regulated competitors, which leads to high prices for consumers and high profits for the regulated industry. Agencies regulating health and safety have been accused of minimizing hazards, failing to set rigorous health and safety standards, and tolerating industry violations of health and safety laws. According to some critics, the central failure of the regulatory system has been its refusal to carry out the public goals of regulation. If these observations are correct, the regulatory system appears as a giant (and expensive) hoax, offering symbolic protection to the public but little real protection from the abuses regulation was meant to prevent.

Before discussing the causes and consequences of capture, a definition of agency capture will be needed. In other words, what should one look for in order to determine whether an agency is captured?

Defining Agency Capture

Perhaps the most straightforward and parsimonious definition of agency capture is that offered by Anderson (1982:484), who defines an agency as captured if "the policies pursued generally coincide with the preference previously expressed by those being regulated." Capture is inferred from the result. The process through which agency policies and industry preferences converge is not specified, though Anderson clearly assumes that industry power has operated to influence agency policy.

A somewhat more elaborate definition is offered by Sabatier (1975), who identifies three different categories of regulatory outcomes from which capture may be inferred. First, a captured agency is one in which the goals the agency chooses result in little economic disruption of the regulated industry, and regulatory policies are designed so that they do not hurt the industry's profitability. Second, a captured agency operates with minimal regulations which are lenient and acceptable to the regulated industry. Third, enforcement is lenient. When violations are discovered, the agency gives the violating firm substantial time to correct the violation, makes frequent exceptions to the rules, and relies upon persuasion rather than coercion to attain compliance. When formal action is used, penalties are very light.

These definitions raise several conceptual problems. First, they assume that something like a unified "industry interest" can be identified. Second, they assume that this "industry interest" is necessarily in conflict with some as yet unidentified, and equally unified, "public interest." Third, by assuming that industry influence is the cause of the observed result, these definitions ignore other explanations for the convergence of industry preferences and agency policy.

Assuming that "industry" is a united front ignores the many examples of industries that include a diverse set of interests, such that policies that are in the interest of one sector of the industry may hurt another sector. In the Wisconsin Department of Agriculture, for example, the kinds of regulations and enforcement policies that are beneficial to dairy farmers are often not in the best interest of cheesemakers. For example, strict enforcement of bacteria levels, such as mastistis, at the farm level hurts farmers but saves cheesemakers money. If industry is not unified, it raises the possibility that the agency may be captured by one segment of the industry, as when the established airlines captured the CAB, effectively limiting competition from new airlines on interstate routes. Another possibility, however, is that the conflicting interest of industry creates the kind of countervailing pressures that are needed to "keep the agency honest" and prevent capture.

The second problem with these definitions is that they assume that industry interests are necessarily in conflict with the broader interests of the public. While certainly this is often the case, there are instances in which private interests may actually coincide with the public interest. For example, since food processing is inherently risky, manufacturers must take precautions and maintain sanitary standards to avoid problems which might ruin their product's reputation or expose the company to civil liability. Through regulation, some of the costs of surveillance and quality control are borne by a public agency rather than by the private company. Moreover, government regulation assures businesses that all operators are required to meet the same minimal standards, so that unfair competitive advantages cannot be enjoyed by companies cutting corners on sanitation and food safety. Definitions of agency capture frequently ignore these kinds of overlapping or complementary interests between private enterprises and the public and deny the possibility that policies serving the public interest might not hurt industry in some instances.

Finally, these definitions assume too much by ignoring other potential explanations for the similarity between industry interests and agency actions. For example, Sabatier (1975) defines as captured any agency that follows a voluntary compliance enforcement strategy. While it is undoubtedly true that captured agencies are likely to adopt such an approach, research on regulation has suggested a number of other factors *unrelated to capture* that provide plausible explanations for the adoption of a voluntary compliance approach. For example, agency officials may want to bring formal action more often, but judges frequently dismiss charges or impose only the most lenient penalties, discouraging regulatory officials from using legal action in the future (Bartrip, 1979). Moreover, in the majority of cases violators correct violations without any formal action (Hawkins, 1983; Mileski, 1971). Finally, these researchers argue that a more stringent and legalistic approach would create regulatory unreasonableness with attendant social costs (Bardach and Kagan, 1982). None of these explanations or justifications of lenient enforcement imply any direct influence by industry on the agency. And if the industry has not influenced the agency, the agency cannot be called captured, no matter how much agency policies appear to benefit the industry.

These definitions are liable to error. By assuming that a given result is the consequence of capture, they risk defining as captured agencies in which other processes have operated to create similar outcomes. They can also make the opposite error of defining agencies as not captured when they are, in fact, captured. For example, in those instances in which industry interests and public interests are not frequently in conflict, the agency can be viewed as generally serving public interests. The key to labeling the agency as captured depends upon the agency's action in those rare instances in which industry interests and public interests conflict. If, whenever there is conflict, the agency defers to industry, the agency should be defined as captured. But in instances where such conflicts are rare, these definitions are likely to err by not defining the agency as captured because the definition attends only to the general and usual policies and actions of the agency. In order to correct these defects of the definitions cited here, it is necessary to examine the processes which led to the observed results.

Processes of Capture

A variety of processes have been suggested by scholars of regulatory capture to explain how industry influences an agency's policy and actions. These processes reflect a variety of ways in which agency personnel are coopted, coaxed, or coerced into accepting industry preferences.

Some see it as a process of delivery, in which key agency posts are given to individuals known to possess pro-industry attitudes (Cary, 1967; Stone, 1973). Others view capture as a process of influencing government officials by offering personal inducements (Quirk, 1981:19). To others still, capture is seen as a consequence of overt political influence, in which agency officials are outmaneuvered in political arenas by experienced, well-connected, and well-funded industry lobbyists (Noll, 1971). Finally, some theorists see capture as an extremely subtle process of psychological conversion, in which regulatory officials grow to appreciate industry "needs" and the industry perspective through a long period of personal acquaintance with industry representatives (Bernstein, 1955).

Some observers point to the executive appointment process and note that in many cases it appears that the agency is not "captured" by the industry, but rather delivered on a silver platter (Cary, 1967; Stone, 1973). Appointment of persons known to hold pro-industry attitudes and who have expressed a desire for restrained regulatory action can usually be counted on to be responsive to industry preferences.

Critics of the Reagan administration's regulatory policies have accused the President of delivering agencies to industry by appointing agency officials who are known to agree with industry's perspective (Tolchin and Tolchin, 1983; Claybrook, 1984). James Watt, the former Secretary of the Interior who was widely excoriated by environmentalists, had earlier served as director of the Mountain States Legal Foundation, which was supported by mining and petroleum interests to fight environmental regulations. Thorne Auchter was a construction company executive before being appointed by President Reagan to head the Occupational Safety and Health Administration (Tolchin and Tolchin, 1983: 98).

In some agencies, "delivery" is built into the appointment process. The enabling legislation frequently requires that appointees to a regulatory board be members of the industry regulated by the board. Such requirements increase the likelihood that appointees will bring pro-industry attitudes to their job and that they will hire officials sharing these attitudes. While this may be a sensible arrangement in relation to the service functions of regulatory agencies, it may temper agency officials' enthusiasm in carrying out control functions.

If officials are not initially sympathetic to industry, a variety of personal incentives can be offered by industry to agency officials to persuade them to be more lenient. In rare cases, bribery may be effective. In most cases, however, the incentives are less blatant. Promises of future employment in the regulated industry, for example, may serve as potent incentives.

These processes suggest a "revolving door" between government and industry, through which employees move back and forth between the public and private sectors. Several studies have found that upper-level regulatory officials frequently were employed in the regulated industry prior to working for the agency, or left agency appointments for jobs in the regulated industry (Domhoff, 1979: 33; Green, 1971: 16; but cf., Freitag, 1983; Quirk, 1981: 143-174; Weaver, 1977).

Other observers have emphasized the political pressures that can be brought to bear on an agency. All agencies are dependent upon elected officials. The chief executive (the governor or President) may ask for the resignation of agency officials in executive departments. The legislative branch can pressure the agency through threats of budget cuts and legislative investigations of agency operations. Since industry invests heavily in supporting political candidates and lobbying elected officials, its political clout can be used to put pressure on agency officials.

A stark example of this process is described by Michael Pertschuk, President Carter's appointee to chair the Federal Trade Commission. Pertschuk, an inveterate consumer advocate, came under a hailstorm of political pressure (see Chapter Three). According to Pertschuk (1982: 56), "More and more businessmen concluded, not irrationally, that creeping government encroachment on their autonomy had to be resisted by direct political action." Industry resisted the FTC's pro-consumer initiatives through a massive lobbying campaign. "A procession of diverse business coalitions—united by what the Chamber of Commerce spokesmen proclaimed as a membership in the society of 'victims of the FTC'—engulfed Congress, beseeching it to debar threatened FTC rule making" (Pertschuk, 1982: 73). Congress responded with hearings and legislation forbidding the FTC to pursue particular rule-making proposals, successfully reining in the regulatory exuberance of the FTC. Moreover, having suffered a crushing political defeat, the agency was chastened in its pursuit of future regulatory initiatives.

Political pressure need not be as open and intense as the campaign against the FTC, however. It may appear in seemingly insignificant, but effective, forms. An industry trade representative may call the chair of a legislative committee having oversight over an agency. The industry representative and the legislator are typically well-acquainted. The lobbyist explains how "unreasonable" the agency is being and notes that the industry knows that it can count on the legislator's support. The legislator calls the agency head and says, "What are you up to down there?" and points out that the committee might just look into what the agency is doing come budget time, if not before. Such intervention, though episodic and far from heavyhanded, may be sufficient to temper regulatory zeal (Ripley and Franklin, 1976).

Even more subtle is the process of psychological conversion leading to agency capture. When Marver Bernstein (1955) first coined the term "capture," he was referring to a long-term process of socializing agency officials to be responsive to industry concerns. Bernstein saw capture as a virtually inevitable process of aging (Sabatier, 1975: 303).

> After a time there generally develops a "subtle relationship in which the mores, attitudes, and thinking of those regulated come to prevail in the approach and thinking of many commissioners," until gradually they perceive their "primary mission as the maintenance of the status quo in the regulated industry."

Bernstein was quite correct in calling the process "subtle." Indeed, the subtlety of the process is what makes it so difficult to observe from the outside.

In order to understand the process of capture, one must first appreciate the political climate within which many regulatory agencies operate. Public issues come and go. After a catastrophe or well-publicized scandal, public groups are mobilized to press for regulatory legislation intended to prevent similar disasters from occurring in the future. A regulatory agency is created, or a new mandate given to an existing agency, but the public rarely remains interested long enough to determine whether the agency carries out the legislative intent. Confident that "something will be done" about the problem and distracted by new issues emerging on the political horizon, the public retreats from any active role in monitoring or influencing the regulatory agency. As long as no new catastrophes are brought to the public's attention, the public simply remains unaware and, in a sense, uninterested in what the agency is doing.

The regulated industry, in contrast, is intensely aware and interested in the agency's activities. In most cases, the industry wants to minimize the effects of the regulation. Through close communication and contact, industry exerts a subtle influence on the agency. In contrast, the public is distant and quiet—easily forgotten and ignored. Over time, given the relative absence of any opposing influences, agency officials come to view regulatory problems from an industry perspective.

Industry representatives and agency officials meet frequently. Industry lobbyists frequently "drop by" officials' offices for informal visits. These visits are used as opportunities to get acquainted. Agency officials come to know industry representatives as real people, as friendly people, and as reasonable people. Any stereotypes or preconceptions that officials may have held that members of industry are only interested in profits and cannot be trusted are eventually worn down through this process of getting to know the people behind the image (Ziegler and Baer, 1969; Milbrath, 1963).

Industry representatives also go out of their way to be helpful and constructive. In meetings with officials, they do not continuously demand preferential treatment or berate officials. Rather, they attempt to present their "concerns" about regulatory policy calmly. They also go out of their way to listen to officials' "problems." These problems may relate directly to regulatory policy, or they may be related to management or even personal problems. No matter what the "problem," industry representatives try to be sympathetic and offer assistance.

For example, if the problem is related to regulatory policy, industry representatives may volunteer to serve on an advisory board to explore alternatives for solving the problem. Firms may offer to conduct research on a particular problem, or may volunteer facilities or personnel to help train agency employees. Regulatory officials rarely have enough time or money to accomplish all of their goals. Consequently, the assistance of industry, whether in the form of an offer to draft a proposed rule or to provide statistical information about a particular question, is most welcome.

Industry representatives also lend a sympathetic ear and offer assistance for problems not directly related to the regulation of the industry. Once industry representatives have become friendly acquaintances, they have placed themselves in a position to be sympathetic listeners. Agency officials tell industry representatives about management problems, union difficulties, and their own personal career aspirations and frustrations. They exchange stories about legislators and other government officials.

As a result, agency officials develop a sense of personal identification with industry representatives. When agency policy or actions create some "problem" for industry, industry can count on a sympathetic reception. Industry representatives are known to agency officials; they are trusted. If violations are discovered, agency officials are willing to listen to explanations from industry representatives, and to believe industry representatives when they say they are working on correcting the violation but need more time. Officials will give industry representatives an opportunity to explain their needs, justifications, and solutions.

There is nothing corrupt or improper about giving industry a fair hearing, but one must remember the context within which these interactions take place. The public does not share the opportunity to explain its needs and justifications for taking action. The public simply is not a participant in the regulatory process in the same way that the industry is.

This is not to imply that this process works in industry's favor every time. Some agency officials will be more amenable than others. Some firms in the industry will be better acquainted with officials than others. Sometimes agency officials simply cannot stretch the rules, even for a firm with which they have developed close and amiable ties. In addition, agencies may possess some capacity to resist the processes of capture, if they are motivated to do so. For example, Miles and Bhambri (1983) found that "activist" (pro-consumer protection) insurance commissioners would cultivate interaction with consumer groups as a means of resisting the pressures of the insurance industry.

But industry does not expect to win every time. Industry representatives recognize that agency officials have a job to do. They also recognize, however, that in the long run, officials who have gained an appreciation of industry's perspective will be more inclined to use their discretion in industry's favor.

Even conflicts may be dealt with in a friendly way to contain the level of conflict. The conflict must be kept civilized and non-personal in order to preserve the advantageous personal relationship with agency officials that has been so carefully curried. Only when the conflict has begun to spiral out of control will industry representatives begin to play "hardball" by withdrawing rewards and engaging in coercive tactics, risking a permanent breach between the industry and the agency.

Through this subtle process of influence and psychological conversion, the independence of agency officials is gradually undermined. Their actions frequently benefit industry at the public's expense. Their goals are re-defined. Minimal protections are viewed as adequate. Serious deficiencies in the regulatory program remain unnoticed by regulatory officials as long as no one points them out. Regulatory officials view their role as one of helping industry, as industry, in turn, helps the regulatory agency. Agency officials see no conflict between industry's goals and the public interest. To the extent that a conflict does in fact exist, the public loses.

Active Cooptation of Industry Power

The processes of capture described by Bernstein and others conceptualize the regulatory agency as passive, responding to pressures exerted by industry. A somewhat different perspective of agency capture conceptualizes the agency as actively pursuing opportunities for coopting industry in order to stabilize the agency's organizational environment. Philip Selznick (1948) has developed some important ideas underscoring the importance of the organizational environment of the regulatory agency and the impact of that environment in shaping the behavior of regulatory agencies.

The conventional analyses of agency capture, described above, focus on the one-sided political environment of captured agencies as distorting agency officials' perspective and influencing their action. In contrast, the cooptation view acknowledges conflict within the regulatory environment and focuses on the regulatory agency's efforts to navigate between the shoals of conflicting imperatives.

In this view, the regulatory environment is complex, including both pro-regulation and anti-regulation politicians, business groups, public advocacy groups, and the media. In the capture view, anti-regulation politicians and business groups are assumed to be so powerful and so dominant in the regulatory environment that regulatory officials need not attend to the interests of opposing groups. In the cooptation view, regulatory officials are painfully aware of their vulnerability to criticism from a variety of sources holding conflicting values and interests in relation to regulatory policy.

It is in light of these forces of conflict that the discussion of cooptation is framed. Selznick (1948: 34) notes that "Cooptation is the process of absorbing new elements into the leadership or policy-determining structure of an organization as a means of averting threats to its stability or existence." The agency engages in cooptation efforts in order to stabilize its environment and deal with potential threats. Cooptation is an organizational defense mechanism for defusing potential conflicts by bringing potentially threatening elements into the policy-making functions of the agency.

As we have seen, regulatory agencies are frequently created in the wake of a scandal that creates a pro-regulation reform movement. At the same time, however, business interests may remain steadfastly opposed to these regulatory efforts. In effect, the agency has not won the "consent of the governed." If the regulated industry does not consent to the authority and control of the regulatory agency, serious conflict emerges in the environment of the regulated agency. According to Selznick (1948: 34), "When control lacks an adequate measure of consent, it may revert to coercive measures or attempt to win the consent of the governed."

Our description of the pro-regulation reform movement of the 1970s and the resulting legalistic policies of enforcement agencies during that era provides an example of using coercive measures to overcome industry resistance. Another possible response of the regulatory agency, however, is to attempt to win over the regulated industry by coopting elements of industry into the leadership and policy-making of the agency.

Selznick (1948: 34) maintains that "cooptation may be a response to the pressures of specific centers of power." Special interests with sufficient power are able to threaten the stability of the regulatory agency. In order to avert these threats, regulatory officials may actively engage in attempts to share power with those groups or individuals that pose the threat in an attempt to avert the "trouble" those individuals or groups could create for the agency.

Where capture views agencies as passively reacting to threats and penetrations from the outside, cooptation views the process as an active and conscious effort on the part of an agency to recruit threatening segments into its ranks. Because the agency is aware that meeting its responsibilities to the public will likely conflict with the interests of other powerful firms or groups, it actively pursues opportunities for averting criticism and "trouble" before these emerge. Thus, regulatory officials respond as much to the potential power of the regulated industry to create "trouble" as it does to the actual use of power by the industry in its efforts to capture the agency.

The following illustrates the process of cooptation. The Wisconsin Department of Agriculture, Trade, and Consumer Protection licenses bakeries to determine their compliance with sanitation and other requirements. Operation of a bakery without a license is a criminal offense.

A few years back, it became a fad in some parts of the state for people to take cake decorating courses at local community colleges and to begin selling decorated cakes out of their homes. Frequently, these amateur enthusiasts turned entrepreneurs were unaware that their home bakeries were required to be licensed under state law.

Investigators from time to time would come across information leading them to these home bakeries, and would follow up with a personal visit to the home. If the investigator found that the home baker was using the family kitchen to prepare commercial baked goods, the inspector would explain that sanitary requirements and state law proscribed this practice and would ask the person to sign a voluntary consent order to cease and desist the use of the home kitchen for commercial purposes. The typical case resulted in the home baker either abandoning the business or, in some cases, setting up a second "commercial" kitchen in another part of the home and obtaining a license. The "normal" response of the agency to these cases was to handle them informally; prosecution of these home bakers was viewed as unreasonable and inappropriate since the violation occurred out of ignorance and the violators complied with the law after they had been informed. This "normal" practice serves to highlight what happened in one particular instance in which the stability of the agency's organizational environment was threatened.

One Sunday, the newspaper ran a human interest story about a woman who was making beautiful wedding cakes in her home. A local baker spotted the article, cut it out, and mailed it to the agency's central office along with a letter complaining about such unlicensed operators. In response to this complaint from industry, the assistant administrator of the agency issued a memorandum directing the regional supervisor for that area to investigate. More importantly, the assistant administrator specified the course of action the regional supervisor should take in dealing with this issue. It is these directives that illustrate cooptation at work.

The assistant administrator's memo stated:

Please investigate this case to determine if the party is licensed. I would suggest that we move rather cautiously in determining the Department's course of action. If [the home baker mentioned in the newspaper article] is not licensed, you may wish to discuss the possibility of the district attorney contacting her concerning obtaining a license or the possibility of signing a complaint. If a complaint is signed, please keep in mind that the district attorney and local bakeries in the county must be in support of it.

If the district attorney or the bakeries in the county are not in support of signing a complaint, then I would suggest we dispense with the case by a certified warning letter from your office.

The assistant administrator appears to be giving a prescription for cooptation. If local bakeries might create trouble in relation to the agency's policies toward unlicensed home bakers, coopt the local bakers by asking their opinion of what the agency should do. The memorandum directs the regional supervisor to determine the will of local bakers in carrying out action on this case.

Cooptation such as this occurs when agency officials perceive segments within the agency's organizational environment as capable of causing "trouble." Interestingly, it is the agency's *perceptions* of the potential for trouble, more than the industry's actual likelihood or ability to cause trouble, that leads to cooptation. In the example above, the letter from a vexed baker was sufficient to unnerve agency officials, resulting in this attempt to coopt the bakers by including them in the decision-making process.

One problem with cooptation, of course, relates to the fairness and appropriateness of regulatory action stemming from such efforts. This home baker faced consequences that were not "normal" in terms of the agency's past practice. The action taken on the case would not be based on the same criteria that were otherwise applied. The potential for discriminatory action is apparent.

Again, cooptation is a defense reaction designed to reduce conflict in an environment that is perceived as hostile or threatening to the status quo. While industry groups may engage in lobbying and influence efforts, such as those described as capture, agencies may also actively engage in appeasement efforts to win the consent of industry to agency authority. This is what we have described here as cooptation.

Consequences of Capture and Cooptation

The definitions of agency capture offered above are based in part on the results or consequences of these processes. These are, perhaps, only the most obvious consequences of agency capture. A number of more subtle effects may also result, including cost-ineffectiveness, lower morale, discriminatory action, industry cynicism, loss of public confidence, and episodic shake-ups.

Because a captured agency requires staff and facilities, just like a non-captured agency, the public is spending money for regulation, but getting little more than industry would do voluntarily without government supervision. Agency capture therefore, is cost-ineffective. Put another way, the public is not getting its money's worth.

Capture also may undermine the morale of lower-level employees, further decreasing agency effectiveness. As noted above, inspectors and other agency personnel frequently pursue these sorts of jobs because they want to serve and protect the public. When they are prevented from doing so, when they feel as though their hands have been tied, and can see no justification for it, they become embittered and cynical. Some simply quit, in which case the agency loses valuable talent and experience. Others may try for a time to change the agency from within. They are likely to come under heavy pressure to conform to agency norms and administrative authority. Finally, many just give up. In its worst form, this loss of morale manifests itself in laziness and even corruption. More typically, inspectors simply lose initiative. As one inspector put it, "If administrators don't care, why should I?"

The cynicism of agency personnel is a reflection of the cynicism of industry. While many firms will continue to "play the game," behaving like relatively "good apples" and maintaining good working relationships with lower-level employees, such as inspectors, some firms flout the inspector's authority and show off their power to make administrators reverse inspector's decisions. This cynicism is also evident in some corporate managers' reactions when inspectors attempt to take enforcement action. They assume that inspectors are picking on them.

This presumption is reinforced by the captured agency's tendency to play favorites. When discretionary decisions are made on the basis of personal relationships and a firm's capacity to "make trouble" for the agency, some firms will receive more preferential treatment than others. Discriminatory action by the agency further erodes the industry's respect for the agency, at the same time that many firms in the industry benefit from it.

How long a situation such as this can continue without coming to light is difficult to predict. In many cases, however, captured agencies appear to experience periodic scandals which temporarily shake things up. The media play a particularly important role in this process. Some scandal, whether discriminatory action or widespread inaction by the agency, is brought to the attention of the media, which then investigates and puts the agency under intense, but usually short-lived, scrutiny. The results of these episodic shake-ups are likely to include a sound drubbing of agency administrators, budget cuts, scapegoating of agency inspectors, perhaps a few firings, but no real change in the agency or its environment (Kemp, 1984).

The long-term result of these periodic scandals and shake-ups is likely to be a loss of public confidence. The public comes to share the cynacism of agency personnel and industry, and the word "inspector" becomes a joke.

The sum of these negative effects is a legitimacy crisis for the captured agency. A governmental agency cannot function when it has lost legitimacy. This loss can be remedied only if the public perceives the agency to be politically accountable, effective, and fair (Freedman, 1978: 11). The question remains: how can these objectives be attained? How can agencies be insulated from industry pressure and capture? How can the regulatory agency protect its legitimacy?

Preventing Capture

One of the basic values underlying administrative law is the concern for representation and the right to be heard. The democratic priniciples underlying the administrative process are intended to assure equal access to government. Government agencies, in turn, have a responsibility to be responsive to all segments of society, corporations and individual citizens alike. The problem in regulatory capture is that the agency is highly responsive to the needs of industry, but is no longer sufficiently responsive to the needs of those citizens regulations were designed to protect. In order to prevent capture, what is needed is a regulatory structure that can be responsive to the legitimate needs of industry (Bardach and Kagan, 1982) while remaining accountable to the public and effective in attaining the goals of regulation.

Recommendations for preventing capture must acknowledge the variety of processes through which agencies are captured. Some of these processes are relatively easy to break. Others are far more difficult.

A number of "clean government" reforms have sought to decrease the opportunities for capture. In some cases, laws prevent agency officials from representing industry in regulatory matters for several years after they have left government jobs (5 CFR 737). Government ethics laws prohibit agency officials from accepting gifts, free lunches, or other things of value from members of industry (5 CFR 735.202). It is unlikely, however, that eliminating these overt forms of influence will significantly alter industry's capacity to influence regulatory decisions.

The most significant impact is likely to occur when the agency's environment is altered to include public representation. Both the "hardball" processes of political pressure and the "softsoap" method of psychological conversion depend on the lack of active public representation. This one-sided political environment allows industry to be not only the most effective voice heard by politicians and agency officials, but the only voice heard. Significant strides toward more vigorous regulation were achieved during the 1970s when public interest groups organized and applied countervailing pressure on government officials. The underlying motivation of the consumer movement and the environmental movement has been the assumption that, left to their own devices, industry in tandem with regulatory agencies would sell the public interest short. An active public is not so easily ignored or discounted by politicians and agency officials.

The prospects of increasing public participation in regulatory decision-making remain somewhat limited, however. The vastness of the regulatory establishment—the incredible number of regulatory agencies and the variety of subjects being regulated—poses an overwhelming challenge. It is unrealistic to hope that enough people can be actively involved in public interest groups to maintain a credible presence in the scores of local, state, and federal regulatory agencies. While periodically historical and political conditions may coalesce to create pro-regulatory movements, like the environmental movement, the majority of regulatory activities remain untouched by these episodic surges in public participation.

If public non-participation is a basic fact of political life, the prospects of preventing capture become quite dim. But if a cure for regulatory capture may be out of our reach, it may yet be possible to institute reforms that will remedy some of the worst symptoms. We should look first at the reform agenda of the consumer, labor, and environmental movements of the 1970s. These reforms dramatically transformed agencies that had become moribund through capture. In other words, they worked.

But these reforms also had their costs, including reduced flexibility, increased legalism, and political counter-attack. These reforms need to be reexamined to find ways of providing for the benefits of these reforms while avoiding the excesses of legalism. Some potential suggestions include more specific statutory enactments, restructuring authority and discretion in regulatory agencies to create organizational safety valves against excessive industry pressure, and professionalization of agency personnel.

More Specific Statutory Enactments

The architects of the regulatory legislation of the 1960s and 1970s recognized that broad regulatory discretion provides an opportunity for agency capture. Public interest groups were actively involved in lobbying for reform legislation and supported provisions that specified regulatory goals and standards for regulatory agencies. For example, the 1958 Delaney Amendment to the Food, Drug, and Cosmetic Act removed FDA's discretion regarding suspected carcinogens. Under the Delaney Amendment, any food additive found to cause cancer in humans or laboratory animals must be banned from use. Environmentalists pushed for legislation that prescribed deadlines for the regulation of air and water pollution. For example, the Clean Air Act mandates timetables for the promulgation of standards relating to specific pollutants, thereby restricting the discretion of agency officials. Provisions of the Occupational Safety and Health Act and the Surface Mining Reclamation and Control Act limit agency discretion in enforcement actions, imposing mandatory penalties for certain categories of violations. These provisions reflect more than a "get tough" attitude. They reduce the degrees of freedom of regulatory officials and narrow the opportunities for agency capture. Of course, by decreasing agency discretion, one also limits the agency's opportunities to use good discretion and to be flexible. Such provisions have come under harsh criticism in recent years, especially from industry. Industry claims that these provisions have resulted in regulatory unreasonableness because agency officials are unable to take exceptional circumstances into account.

Structuring Authority and Discretion

In most regulatory agencies, and particularly in captured agencies, lower-level employees, such as investigators, researchers, inspectors, and their immediate supervisors, possess little authority. Most regulatory action must be cleared in advance by upper-level agency officials. The most common justifications for this organization of authority is that it promotes consistency in regulatory action and allows upper-level officials, who have a view of the entire program, to direct scarce resources to the highest priority concerns. In fact, one of the leading scholars of administrative law has conceptualized the main challenge of agency managers to be controlling the discretion of lower-level employees (see Davis, 1960).

Our examination of agency capture, however, reveals that it is not the discretion of lower level employees that needs to be controlled. Rather, it is the discretion of agency managers. Close examination reveals that upper-level officials' decisions are frequently inconsistent and their actions reflect questionable priorities.

In these cases, the limitation on lower-level employees' authority serves an additional function. Where authority is concentrated in a few hands, regulated firms can focus their efforts at cooptation on those few individuals and effectively capture the entire agency. Agency managers, in turn, use their discretion to avoid enforcement in cases in which inspectors recommend that formal enforcement action be taken. If administrators hold the power to check inspectors' authority, and there is no countervailing check on the administrator's discretion, capture of the administrators is equivalent to capture of the agency.

The solution to this problem is to transform the structure of authority in these agencies so that lower-level employees are free to take necessary action, without those decisions running into political interference. At the same time, the solution must attend to the valid managerial concerns of promoting consistency and regulatory priorities.

One solution is to establish guidelines which guide the authority and discretion of lower-level employees, but without allowing agency managers to interfere in cases that might create "trouble." If a case fits within the established guidelines, the case could proceed without having to obtain specific approval from agency managers. Managers' priorities would already be reflected in the guidelines, and application of the guidelines would achieve the necessary consistency from one inspector to the next. As long as the case falls within the established guidelines, managers should be constrained from interfering in the actions initiated by inspectors. If an inspector wished to recommend legal action in a case that did not fall within the guidelines, such cases might be forwarded to agency managers for a case-by-case review. If a large number of cases were forwarded for review, it would be an indication that the guidelines were in need of revision.

A system of guidelines would eliminate the opportunity of upper-level managers to exercise "bad discretion," which we have suggested is one of the primary consequences of agency capture. This is essentially a managerial reform, affecting the structure of authority within the regulatory agency as an organization. We turn now to some additional questions relating to successfully managing the regulatory bureaucracy to guard against capture.

Professionalization of Agency Personnel

Professionalization may provide another means of inoculating the agency against capture. Professionalization involves both education concerning the technical aspects of regulation as well as socialization to professional norms and values, and a professional mission.

One goal of professionalization, then, is simply to upgrade the technical competence and expertise of agency personnel, from the inspector in the field to the top administrators. As we have seen, in agencies that are vulnerable to agency capture, lack of technical knowledge can result in agency personnel backing off from enforcement action because they are unsure whether there is a violation or whether it is serious. Impressed by the technical credentials of a firm's own compliance specialists, a poorly trained inspector or administrator may be convinced that the firm's justifications for the violation are valid. Rather than coming to their own decision on the basis of evidence, technically incompetent personnel will rely on the expert opinion of industry.

A second goal of professionalization is to impart values. The process of regulatory capture is in many cases a process of education and socialization, in which regulatory officials are socialized to the values and perspectives of the regulated industry. Professionalization may provide an alternative avenue for reinforcing values consistent with protecting the public. A professional commitment to the advocacy of public goals in rule-making and to the law enforcement role may create a countervailing set of values, insulating officials from the process of psychological conversion.

Professionalization involves an on-going involvement with professional groups. Through continuing education programs and professional association meetings, professional values are reinforced. Officials have an opportunity to renew their commitment to values which may temper the messages communicated by industry.

Conclusion

The concept of agency capture assumes conflict between industry and the public interest. When an agency is captured, industry wins almost every time. Captured agencies follow policies that do not threaten to disrupt the profitability of regulated firms. More ambitious regulatory goals are abandoned, regardless of the potential benefits to the public, if they would cost industry "too much." Regulations are weak, often corresponding to the industry's own voluntary standards, and, consequently, are acceptable to industry. A captured agency does not undertake bold new regulatory initiatives. In addition, the captured agency is a lenient enforcer of regulations. When violations are discovered, violators are given ample time to correct them without penalty. In those rare cases in which the agency does pursue enforcement, penalties are light (Sabatier, 1975).

Activists, politicians, and scholars continue to debate whether regulatory agencies have become the captives of the industries they are supposed to regulate. Some look at the same regulatory behavior that the critics do, and find nothing wrong. Rather than viewing these agencies as captured, they view agency policies favoring industry as part of the normal give-and-take of policy-making and view the agencies as properly responsive to the needs of industry.

Which group of observers is correct? That is precisely the problem. Few issues in regulation are as difficult as the concept of "agency capture." Although it is fairly easy to describe what is meant by "capture," it becomes difficult, and perhaps impossible, to demonstrate that a particular agency is captured or that a great many agencies are captured. No scientific formulae exist to determine whether an agency is using "good" discretion or "bad" discretion and whether regulatory policies are serving broad, public interests or narrow, private interests. These are questions of judgment.

Consequently, for every agency that some observers would label captured, others would deny capture, offering rational explanations for agency policies that appear to benefit the industry at the expense of the public. These ambiguities are, frankly, insoluble. The most reasonable procedure is to closely examine an agency's record, to uncover any influence exerted by industry on agency policy, and to present all of the evidence so that others may draw their own conclusions.

To the extent that capture actually occurs, its principal cause appears to lie in the one-sided ideological and political environment in which most regulatory officials find themselves and their need to obtain the consent of industry through cooptation. Therefore, the best antidote to regulatory capture would be for a diversity of interests to be represented before the agency in both formal and informal contacts. Since this is unlikely to occur, other stop-gap remedies for capture must be relied on, including statutory limits on regulatory discretion, professionalization of regulatory personnel, and diffusion of regulatory authority. Before such remedies are likely to be instituted, however, regulatory capture must be perceived as a prevalent and serious social problem.

References

Anderson, James E. (1982) "The Public Utility Commission of Texas: A Case of Capture or Rapture?" *Policy Studies Review* 1: 484-490.

Bardach, Eugene and Robert A. Kagan (1982) *Going by the Book: The Problem of Regulatory Unreasonableness.* Philadelphia: Temple University Press.

Bartrip, Peter W.J. (1979) "Safety at Work: The Factory Inspectorate in the Fencing Controversy, 1833-1857." Working Paper No. 4. Oxford: Social Science Research Council.

Bernstein, Marver (1955) *Regulation of Business by Independent Commission*. Princeton, NJ: Princeton University Press.

Cary, William L. (1967) *Politics and the Regulatory Agencies*. New York: McGraw-Hill.

Claybrook, Joan (1984) *Retreat from Safety: Reagan's Attack on America's Health*. New York: Pantheon.

Davis, Kenneth Culp (1960) *Administrative Law and Government*. St. Paul, MN: West Publishing.

Domhoff, G. William (1979) *The Powers that Be: Processes of Ruling Class Domination in America*. New York: Vintage Books.

Freedman, James O. (1978) *Crisis and Legitimacy*. New York: Cambridge University Press.

Freitag, Peter J. (1983) "The Myth of Corporate Capture: Regulatory Commissions in the United States." *Social Problems* 30: 480-491.

Green, Mark (1973) *The Monopoly Makers: Ralph Nader's Study Group Report on Regulation and Competition*. New York: Grossman.

Hawkins, Keith (1983) "Bargain and Bluff: Compliance Strategy and Deterrence in the Enforcement of Regulation." *Law and Policy Quarterly* 5: 35-73.

Kemp, Kathleen (1984) "Accidents, Scandals, and Political Support for Regulatory Agencies." *Journal of Politics* 46: 401-427.

Milbrath, Lester (1963) *The Washington Lobbyists*. Chicago: Rand McNally.

Miles, Robert H. and Arvind Bhambri (1983) *The Regulatory Executives*. Beverly Hill: Sage Publications.

Mileski, Maureen (1971) *Policing Slum Landlords: An Observation of Administrative Control*. Ph.D. dissertation, Yale University.

Noll, Roger G. (1971) "The Behavior of Regulatory Agencies." *Review of Social Economy* 19: 15-19.

Pertschuk, Michael (1982) *Revolt Against Regulation: The Rise and Pause of the Consumer Movement.* Los Angeles: University of California Press.

Quirk, Paul J. (1981) *Industry Influences in Federal Regulatory Agencies.* Princeton, NJ: Princeton University Press.

Ripley, Randall B. and Grace A. Franklin (1976) *Congress, the Bureaucracy, and Public Policy.*

Sabatier, Paul (1975) "Social Movements and Regulatory Agencies: Toward a More Adequate—and Less Pessimistic—Theory of 'Clientele Capture.'" *Policy Sciences* 6: 301-342.

Selznick, Philip (1948) "Foundations of the Theory of Organization." *American Sociological Review* 13: 25-35.

Stone, Alan (1973) "The FTC and Advertising Regulation." *Public Policy* 21: 203-234.

Tolchin, Susan and Martin Tolchin (1983) Dismantling America: *The Rush to Deregulate.* Boston: Houghton Mifflin.

Weaver, Suzanne (1977) *Decision to Prosecute: Organization and Public Policy in the Antitrust Division.* Cambridge, MA: MIT Press.

Ziegler, Harmon L. and Michael A. Baer (1969) *Lobbying: Interaction and Influence in American State Legislatures.* Belmont, CA: Wadsworth.

CHAPTER 7

The Road to Reform

Our portrait of the regulatory system may appear rather bleak. It seems as though regulatory agencies need to be controlled at least as much the corporations that the agencies are supposed to be controlling. In Chapter 6 we suggested some reforms to counter agency capture, which we consider to be one of the foremost causes of regulatory failure. But agency capture is not the only criticism of regulation and regulatory agencies. In recent years, the bookstores and professional journals have been filled with titles offering diagnoses of regulatory failure and prescriptions for reform. Our purpose here is to review those that we find most thought-provoking or promising, and to add a few thoughts of our own.

Controlling Regulatory Extravagance

One of the central criticisms brought in recent years by economists and corporate managers is that the regulatory system has become too expensive. Regulatory agencies, they say, have gone on such a rule-making rampage that the costs of complying with regulations have skyrocketed. Our economy can not support such high levels of regulatory extravagance.

Litan and Nordhaus (1983:4) draw an analogy between regulatory rule-making and more direct expenditures and taxation by the government.

> From an economic viewpoint, federal regulations are akin to federal expenditure programs. Both require that resources be expended to the pursuit of objectives the nation collectively deems to be important. The only difference is that, in the case of federal expenditures, the resources are first collected through taxation and then spent directly by the government. In the case of regulation, the government orders individuals or firms in the private sector to make such expenditures....

The problem, according to Litan and Nordhaus, is that while there is an elaborate and publicly accountable system for coordinating taxation and appropriation through the legislative process, up to now no similar system of coordination and oversight exists in regard to regulatory "expenditures."

Litan and Nordhaus argue that the solution is a regulatory budget. By placing upper limits on the amount of money that could be spent, both publicly and privately, a regulatory budget would require legislators and regulatory administrators to make choices regarding the allocation of resources. In addition, the regulatory budget process would provide an opportunity for regulatory initiatives to be assessed in relation to other regulatory options.

According to Litan and Nordhaus (1983: 134-135), in order for the regulatory budget to achieve these objectives, the budget procedure must include three key features. The budget must impose dollar restraints on the amount of money which regulations force private firms to expend. Second, like the fiscal budget, the regulatory budget procedure should involve both the executive and the legislative branches. Third, the regulatory budget procedure must include a sanction provision for sanctioning agencies which exceed their budgetary limits.

One of the key drawbacks to the regulatory budget reform proposal is the difficulty of obtaining reliable estimates of the amount of money actually spent by private firms in complying with regulations. Litan and Nordhaus (1983: 152) cite examples of the large discrepancies in cost estimates which the budget process is likely to encounter.

> In 1978 the Consumer Product Safety Commission estimated the direct compliance cost of a proposed fabric flammability regulation for the furniture industry at $57 to $87 million a year. The American Textile Manufacturers Institute, in contrast, estimated direct compliance cost at $1.3 billion per year.

> In 1978 the Environmental Protection Agency estimated the annual direct compliance costs of a proposed ambient air quality standard for ozone at $6.9 to $9.5 billion per year. The RARG estimated those direct compliance costs at $14.3 to $18.8 billion per year.

> In February 1979, the Environmental Protection Agency estimated the costs of a proposed 1981 diesel engine particulate standard at a negative $160 per ton of particulates removed. The council on Wage and Price Stability estimated this cost at a positive $4,740. For a proposed 1983 standard, the estimates per ton were $3,200 and $7,650, respectively.

Besides extremely wide ranges in the estimates, industry has a vested interest in overstating the expected costs of compliance (Nader, 1980: 78). As in the above examples, industry estimates are consistently larger than the cost estimates produced by the regulatory agencies.

Finally, a regulatory budget must also account for the benefits produced; in other words, it should measure only the net costs of compliance. But measuring the benefits of regulation has proved to be even more difficult than measuring the costs (Frank, 1985; Litan and Nordhaus, 1983). Because of these problems, the regulatory budget may seek to operate at a level of precision that is not attainable in reality.

Creating New Sanctioning Alternatives

Because of the supposed inefficiency of criminal sanctions, combined with dissatisfaction with the traditional administrative sanctions that are available to regulatory agencies, a number of scholars have proposed some "new ideas" for controlling corporate illegality. A number of these proposals concern penalties and other remedies that might be used to gain greater control over corporate behavior.

The search for additional or novel sanctions for controlling corporations stems primarily from the belief that monetary fines are inadequate to deter firms from violating the law (Fisse and French, 1985). To provide more meaningful deterrents, scholars have turned their attention to such sanctions as equity fines and publicity. Others have been more concerned with finding rehabilitative alternatives, such as probation and community service orders.

Equity fines, or stock dilution, was first suggested by Coffee (1981) as a means of imposing large, non-monetary fines. The corporation is required to issue new stock amounting to some percentage of the total shares currently issued by the corporation. These new shares would be issued to a public organization, which could retain the stock or sell it at the current cash value.

The main advantage of the equity fine is that it avoids the "deterrence trap" which occurs when corporations do not have sufficient cash to pay a fine that is proportional to the gravity of the offense. In addition, the cost of the fine is more directly borne by the stockholders, rather than by consumers or employees who are most likely to bear the burdens of a monetary fine (Fisse, 1985: 142). The major disadvantage of the equity fine is that it is not guaranteed to have the deterrent effect it is designed to achieve. Since the expected risk of apprehension and punishment is still a major factor in deterring corporations, it is not clear that equity fines would be any more effective than monetary fines.

Publicity has been suggested for decades as a means of deterring corporate illegality. Some agencies make frequent use of publicity as an informal means of gaining compliance (Heffron and McFeeley, 1983: 204).

> The FDA, for example, used press releases not only to inform the public of the dangers of toxic shock syndrome...but also to pressure Proctor and Gamble to take the 'voluntary' action of withdrawing Rely [a tampon which was associatcd with a large number of toxic shock cases] from the market.

Such informal use of publicity has been criticized because of the potential for wrongfully damaging corporations' reputations through the careless release of incorrect information.

Another approach to the use of publicity that has been suggested is "to make adverse publicity available as a formal court-ordered punitive sanction" (Fisse, 1985: 147-148). Publicity has been hailed as a punishment that cannot be written off as "just another cost of doing business." In addition, by publicizing the illegal acts of corporations, advocates of publicity orders argue, corporations would be subjected to public shame and loss of corporate prestige. Fisse and Braithwaite (1983) found that some corporate executives were very concerned about the potential of negative publicity damaging corporate prestige, which suggests that it may serve as a genuine deterrent.

Other novel sanctioning approaches reject the deterrence model. Rather than trying to influence corporate conduct by threatening sanctions, and hoping that these affect corporate decision-making, probation and other controls on corporate management have been suggested as a means of getting "inside" the corporation. Through conditions on probation, judges can require organizational reforms and internal discipline and auditing procedures, as well as appointing a "probation officer" with full access to corporate records, staff and communications (see Fisse, 1985; Braithwaite, 1985: 167).

Community service orders have been suggested as a means of providing some restitution for harms which corporate illegality creates. Such orders have been used in at least two major corporate crime cases in the United States (Fisse, 1985: 149). "A community service sanction . . . would require corporate defendants to undertake a socially useful program involving a commitment of time, effort, and available skills" (Fisse, 1985: 149). For example, six bakeries convicted of price-fixing were required to provide free baked goods to various organizations for the needy for a year (Fisse, 1985:

149). One of the principal objections to community service orders is that they frequently have exactly the opposite result of publicity orders. Rather than decreasing corporate prestige, community service orders create the public impression that the corporation is a model corporate citizen, providing charity of its own free will.

All of these novel approaches are available to judges who wish to expand the armory of sanctions which are available for dealing with corporate illegality. Through probation orders or consent orders, these sorts of sanctions can be imposed even where there is no specific statutory authorization for them. As a practical matter, however, judges and regulatory officials have not gone very far toward experimenting with novel approaches. Nor is it clear that these approaches would be any more effective in practice than the more familiar remedies and penalties on which regulatory officials rely. Nonetheless, the broader the range of potential remedies which officials may seek, the greater flexibility they have in fashioning an appropriate remedy for each individual situation.

Fostering Corporate Responsibility

A number of commentators have suggested that rather than buttressing our regulatory agencies with more power, more sanctions, and more layers of supervising bureaucracy, the answer to controlling corporate illegality may lie in relying less on the law and more on non-governmental forms of social control. Economists are particularly fond of arguments that employ market incentives for controlling corporations, while sociologists stress the need to strengthen the norms for compliance.

Economists, for example, have suggested that instead of relying on command-and-control regulations, corporate behavior might be influenced more indirectly through the use of taxation. The government could tax behaviors that it wished to discourage, or offer tax reductions to those who engage in behaviors that the government wants to encourage. For example, import taxes are used as a means of discouraging people from buying foreign goods. Tax advantages have also been established to encourage individuals and firms to employ energy conservation techniques.

Taxation has also been suggested, though less widely adopted, as an alternative for controlling the kinds of behavior that are usually subject to regulation. For example, a number of economists have suggested that rather than establishing pollution regulations, the government should impose an "effluent tax." The discharges of factories would be measured, and the more the factory discharged, the more tax it would pay. If tax levels were high enough, at least some factories would find it more economical to adopt pollution-control techniques than to pay the tax.

One of most popular proposals for fostering responsibility made by social scientists seeks to create a more effective corporate "conscience" through organizational changes within corporations themselves.   Ralph Nader, for example, has called for the public appointment of outside directors of corporations, whose primary responsibility would be to serve as the superego of the corporation.   Christopher Stone labels this perspective the Interventionist approach.

According to Stone, Interventionists reject the economists' assumption that corporations act like the classical Economic Man.   Instead, Interventionists argue, corporate decision-making is distorted by a variety of non-rational concerns.   If corporations are not the rational actors portrayed by economists, and even some criminologists (Geis, 1972), then the conventional regulatory strategy aimed at deterring violations will not work.

Stone (1985: 17) summarizes the Interventionist approach:

> Instead of trying to daunt the managers into taking appropriate precautions indirectly, through threat of future profit loss, the Interventionist would require a present precaution directly, even to the point of displacing managerial discretion over how the very management system itself is designed.   In effect, the law shifts its emphasis from penalizing outcomes to mandating process.

The law would mandate organizational structures and processes in ways that promote the development and communication of information related to regulatory compliance.   By mandating the collection and organizational dissemination of information, some of the violations that currently occur through corporate oversight would, presumably, be discovered.   Furthermore, by specifying accountability systems within corporations, responsible corporate officers could not shirk their responsibility under the veil of ignorance.

Stone points to some current, if somewhat preliminary, examples of this type of regulatory intervention.   The FDA requires pharmaceutical companies to establish organizational procedures that assure that "responsible corporate officials" be notified in writing of any FDA actions affecting the corporation's products.   Similarly, the Nuclear Regulatory Commission requires that licensees must adopt procedures for informing "responsible officers" of failings and defects (Stone, 1985: 18).   The thrust of the interventionist argument is that these sorts of requirements might be expanded to structure corporations in ways that, first, make them more responsible, and second, establish accountability for those instances in which the corporation acts irresponsibly anyway.

Enforced Self-Regulation

Another suggested reform, which is partly directed toward fostering corporate responsibility, is John Braithwaite's notion of "enforced self-regulation." "The concept of enforced self-regulation is a response both to delay, red tape, costs, and stultification of innovation that can result from imposing detailed government regulations on business, and to the naivete of trusting companies to regulate themselves" (Braithwaite, 1982: 1470). Braithwaite notes the failure of both the criminal justice system and the regulatory justice system in controlling corporate crime. He places a great deal of emphasis on the costs of government regulation and assumes that the government will never have sufficient funds to do an adequate job of surveillance and enforcement on its own (Braithwaite, 1982:1466-1467).

In addition to the limitations of government surveillance and enforcement, he notes several advantages of self-regulation. He cites instances in which private inspection by industry groups have resulted in more frequent and more in-depth investigations and inspections and were conducted by inspectors with better training than government inspectors (Braithwaite, 1982: 1468-1469).

Many companies and industries maintain their own internal compliance and inspection programs. The problem with relying on this self-regulation, of course, is that while corporations may be more capable of policing themselves than the government, "they are not necessarily more willing to regulate effectively" (Braithwaite, 1982: 1469). For Braithwaite, this situation posed a challenge. How might one take advantage of the corporation's inherently greater ability to discover violations? How might corporations be motivated to use this ability, even in those cases where complying is likely to cost money? Braithwaite's answer is enforced self-regulation.

In a nutshell, enforced self-regulation involves reforms in both the rule-making and enforcement processes of the regulatory system. The government would require each company to write a detailed set of rules, tailored to the circumstances facing that company. This aspect of the proposal is designed to eliminate some of the problems encountered when regulatory agencies attempt to write detailed rules relating to a multitude of different situations occurring in the corporations under regulation. The individualized rules would eliminate vagueness and site-level unreasonableness at the same time that it increased the perceived legitimacy of the rules. After all, if the company itself writes the rules, it is difficult for them to claim, at a later date, that the rules are unreasonable. The government would approve the rules on a case-by-case basis, sending back for revision any rules that the agency considered insufficiently stringent to meet the goals of regulation. As in the normal rule-making process, interested parties would have an opportunity to comment on the proposed rules.

The second aspect of enforced self-regulation relates to enforcement. Under Braithwaite's proposal, most enforcement duties would be carried out by the regulated firm. Each firm would be required to establish a regulatory compliance group. The role of government inspectors would be directed primarily toward assuring that the compliance group is organizationally independent, with the authority to take necessary compliance action. Government inspectors would also conduct periodic audits to assure that the compliance group was doing its work and was being appropriately tough.

The compliance group would have a legal responsibility to report to management any violations it discovers. If managers comply with the compliance group's directives, the entire matter is handled internally. No public record that the violation existed would be made, no report of the violation would be made to the regulatory agency, and no publicity would accompany discovery of the violation. If, on the other hand, corporate managers overruled the directives of the compliance group, the compliance group would have a legal obligation to report the violation to the regulatory agency. Following this report, the regulatory agency would take action to force compliance.

Braithwaite cites a number of advantages to be gained through his proposal of enforced self-regulation. Companies would be more committed to obey rules they wrote themselves. Given the greater ability of corporate inspectors to discover violations, more violations would be identified. Corporations would bear more of the costs of regulation because the compliance group would be company employees rather than public employees. Offenders who were caught would be subject to internal discipline more often than when government inspectors discover violations, since government regulation creates an incentive for corporations to cover-up for their employees rather than holding them responsible. In addition, government enforcement of those violations reported to the agency would be improved. The greater precision in the individualized rules would make prosecution easier, and the compliance group's report would provide a powerful piece of evidence against the company. Finally, Braithwaite predicts, compliance would become the "path of least resistance" under enforced self-regulation. Since violations that are corrected remain private, while those that are not corrected would become public through the compliance group's report, corporate managers should have strong incentives to follow the directives of the compliance group.

In spite of these advantages, Braithwaite is not blind to some potentially serious drawbacks to his proposal. He notes that it might lead to unfair scapegoating of employees as managers attempt to pin the blame on subordinates. More importantly, the independence of the compliance group cannot be guaranteed. If enforced self-regulation is to work, the compliance group must be free to issue directives and to report non-compliance to the regulatory agency.

Braithwaite notes a number of ways in which the independence of the compliance group can be undermined. First, as corporate employees, the compliance group may have such a strong sense of corporate loyalty that they do not make any recommendations or directives that are likely to be very costly to the corporation. Instead, they subordinate regulatory goals to profit goals.

In addition, the corporation itself may take steps to undermine the independence and effectiveness of the compliance group. The corporation may decrease budget allocations to the compliance group in retaliation for the group's actions. Managers may shuffle staff around, undermining the competence of compliance group staff. There is good reason to suspect that this might occur. Even corporate managers are skeptical of industry's capacity to regulate itself. Over half of the retired middle-managers interviewed by Clinard (1983: 107) agreed that industry cannot police itself because of greed and unethical conduct by some managers.

Finally, because the compliance group is likely to be housed in the quality control department of the corporation, the compliance group may experience pressure to direct more effort to its quality control functions and less effort toward discovering regulatory violations. If there is a high likelihood that the independence of compliance groups would be undermined, government regulators would have to devote more time and effort to monitoring the stringency and effectiveness of compliance groups. At some point, this oversight function would be hardly distinguishable from routine inspection as it is currently practiced.

Braithwaite admits that enforced self-regulation cannot be viewed as a panacea and may be more workable in some regulatory areas than in others. He concludes by noting (Braithwaite, 1982: 1503-1504):

> The challenge is to find an optimal mix of self-regulation and governmental regulation—a mix that will cover the gaps left by one approach with the strengths of another approach. By exploiting the advantages and recognizing the weaknesses of enforced self-regulation, voluntary self-regulation, and direct governmental regulation, we might strike a mix that is more effec-

tive and less expensive than any one- or two-dimensional approach.

Flexible Enforcement

Although enforced self-regulation has not been instituted in any contemporary regulatory reform efforts, elements of it can be found in the idea of flexible enforcement, which was instituted by the California Occupational Safety and Health Administration and is described by Joseph Rees. Rees offers this case study as an example of flexible enforcement at work.

According to Rees (1986: 3):

> The program's key feature is a jobsite labor-management safety committee (two representatives each from labor and management) that assumes many of OSHA's regulatory responsibilities, such as conducting inspections and investigating complaints. CAL/OSHA, for its part, ceases routine compliance inspections and pursues a more cooperative relationship with these companies.

CAL/OSHA assigns a Designated Compliance Officer (DCO) to each site. Rather than placing the DCO under constraints to write up violations, as other CAL/OSHA inspectors have been in the recent past, the DCOs are free to use a greater degree of flexibility. The DCOs use their authority and enforcement powers to support the jobsite safety engineers who are seeking compliance with regulations. At the same time, however, the DCOs act primarily as consultants and advisors on safety problems. The DCOs spend much of their time educating the labor-management safety team on how to recognize hazards and attempt to foster a cooperative problem-solving approach focused on safety rather than on formalistic rule compliance. The DCO also takes time to explain to the safety team the significance of regulations that may seem irrelevant or downright stupid on the surface.

The results of this program have been quite promising, resulting in a decrease in the number of job accidents on participating sites compared to their performance before the start of the program and to other comparable jobsites. In addition, leading participants from labor and management hailed the program as a success.

The experience with flexible enforcement in the CAL/OSHA program is encouraging. It appears to provide an adequate degree of regulatory protection without engendering the negative side effects of legalistic enforcement. It poses a potential regulatory structure for achieving effective flexible enforcement.

Several caveats are in order, however. First, only those companies with an exemplary in-house safety system for protecting workers were eligible to participate, and participation was purely on a voluntary basis. In other words, these were good apples who chose to participate in the program. Second, the kinds of job hazards that are found on construction sites, which were the only types of jobsites included in this program, may be more easily identified by an internal safety team than hazards found in other job situations. This may be particularly true in relation to health hazards.

Finally, and most importantly, job safety is different from other areas of regulation in that the constituents who will benefit most from effective regulation (workers) are directly involved at the site where the violations take place. In other areas of regulation, such as environmental or consumer safety regulation, there is no analog to the labor-management safety team. Thus, it is questionable whether this suggested reform is generalizable to areas of regulation outside the occupational safety and health area.

Facilitating Interest Group Formation

The problem of attaining regulatory effectiveness hinges not just on the non-availability of on-site constituents to look after their interests and to participate in a form of self-regulation. As we have seen, interest groups supporting regulation and regulatory effectiveness seldom arise with sufficient organization, resources, and momentum to have an impact on regulatory policies. Some suggestions for regulatory reform focus on facilitating the formation of public interest groups and their effective participation in the regulatory process.

At the rule-making stage, one of the suggestions that has been used on a limited basis is the "public intervenor." Because public interest groups have very limited resources with which to make their voices heard by regulatory officials, it has been suggested that the government subsidize some of the costs of participating in the rule-making process. For example, in 1974 the Moss-Magnuson FTC Improvement Act authorized the FTC to pay attorney and expert witness fees as well as the expenses of parties who would otherwise be unable to participate in the rule-making process. Public intervenor funding authority was also given to the Federal Energy Regulatory Commission, the Environmental Protection Agency, the Food and Drug Administration, the Consumer Product Safety Commission, and the Department of Agriculture.

The aim of this reform was to open up the rule-making process, rather than allowing it to be dominated by industry because non-industry groups lacked the funds to participate effectively. The Administrative Procedures

Act formally provides for open proceedings. Public intervenor funding was meant to open the proceedings in practice.

Some industry groups have strongly criticized public intervenor funding, complaining that it is unfair for the government to subsidize special interests and charging that agencies are able to stack the deck by deciding which groups it will subsidize with public intervenor funding. Since 1972, over $2 million has been spent on public intervenors. In the 1980s, however, the tide turned and Congress explicitly prohibited some agencies from providing such funding (Heffron and McFeeley, 1983: 240-241).

Another reform aimed at increasing public participation in rule-making was undertaken by New York State under the mandate of the Environmental Protection Agency in relation to planning construction projects under the Clean Water Act. In particular, this reform specified several mechanisms for increasing citizen participation, including citizen advisory committees, public meetings and formal public hearings. "Underlying the concept of the [Citizens Advisory Committee] is the idea that a group of citizens who meet regularly and represent various interests can constructively affect the decision making process" (Schwartz, 1984: 8). The effectiveness of this mechanism remains unclear pending further study of the 1,000 projects in which it was used in New York State (Schwartz, 1984: 9).

Regulatory administrators who are interested in fostering broader interest group participation can also undertake a variety of informal activities to involve groups of citizens. For example, Miles and Bhambri (1983: 54-55) found that "activist" insurance commissioners took steps to increase the participation of public constituencies. One such activist agency organized a "consumers' conference" to bring together all relevant consumer groups in the state, distribute information, and get feedback from the consumer groups. Such voluntary efforts on the part of regulatory administrators cannot be relied upon, however, as a primary means of fostering broader public involvement.

Facilitating public involvement in the enforcement process is even more challenging than it is in the rule-making process. While some reformers have focused on the idea of the government ombudsman, others have argued that such systems only create another layer of bureaucracy and red tape without significantly altering the pressures which push agencies to downplay the public interest. If more government is not the answer, how can greater balance in the political environment of regulatory agencies be achieved?

We may proceed on the basis of three assumptions. First, there is no reason to hope that the public will become more involved than it has been over the past ten years. During this time, public interest group activity in regulatory matters reached an all-time high. Even so, it was largely confined to a few areas of regulation and heavily focused on federal regulatory efforts. Second, the public favors stricter regulatory action than is achieved when industry dominates the political environment of the agency. And third, the public's day-to-day presence at the agency is not as important as regulatory officials' day-to-day awareness of their accountability to the public and the public's interest in effective regulation.

Fostering this sense of accountability appears to be the key to balancing the regulatory environment. One means of creating an on-going sense of accountability is to professionalize regulatory personnel and to build a professional identification with the public's interest. One source of conflict within regulatory agencies, which we have identified in our own research, stems from the conflicting professional orientations of managers compared to inspectors and other front-line employees. Inspectors and the technical staff undergo a process of professional socialization in which they learn the gravity of the problems which they control through regulation. Consequently, their professional values coincide with the protection of the public. Regulatory managers, on the other hand, are more often professional public administrators rather than professionals in the technical fields related to the area of regulation. They conceptualize their professional role as mediators rather than advocates for the public.

One potential means of creating greater balance in the regulatory environment, therefore, is to require agency managers to have similar professional training and experience as the front-line staff of the agency. This does not mean that regulatory officials will be unresponsive to the interests of industry, but that industry interests are less likely to overwhelm the decision-making process.

Managing for Ideal Enforcement

In Chapter 6, we focused on some of the problems which lead agency managers to abandon any attempt at ideal enforcement, opting instead for discretion which minimizes managers' conflict with industry and favors those firms which have the greatest potential for creating "trouble." We suggested several reforms which could help to insulate agency managers from pressures exerted by industry. But even if managers want to enforce the law fairly, reaching ideal enforcement poses special challenges.

Some of the reform proposals discussed already are important in surmounting these challenges. Enforcement guidelines, the decentralization of authority within agencies, and the professionalization of both field and management staff contribute to the organizational environment that will promote ideal enforcement. A final ingredient is the de-bureaucratization of the regulatory process.

The reforms of the 1970s relied on a heavily bureaucratized model of regulatory agencies. Agencies were to be controlled by placing more and more constraints on their action. The result of these reforms was legalistic enforcement and inflexibility. Rule-compliance overshadowed problem-solving. The long-term consequence of these reforms was to create so much animosity between regulators and the regulated firms that a backlash was created, the effects of which are still being felt today. An alternate organizational model would build on the organizational climate created by decentralization, professionalization, and the creation of guidelines.

Charles Perrow (1970) has shown that some organizational tasks are inherently unsuited to a highly bureaucratized structure. In particular, tasks which require that highly trained professionals use a large degree of discretion require an organizational structure that is collegial rather than bureaucratized and hierarchical. Similar observations have been made in regard to a number of government agencies, such as police departments and those agencies which have been dubbed street-level bureaucracies (Brown, 1981; Lipsky, 1980).

A collegial management style, such as one might find in a research laboratory, assumes that managers and staff share similar expertise and professionalism, and that decisions are made jointly. The job of managers is not so much to control staff as to facilitate their work. This sort of orientation could facilitate ideal enforcement (see Frank, 1984).

In this model, management would have two primary functions. First, managers would be responsible for obtaining the resources necessary to do the job. Resources include adequate numbers of trained staff as well as technical and legal specialists to assist with particularly difficult cases. Second, managers would oversee the entire regulatory program, spotting shortcomings and new problems emerging on the horizon, bringing these to the staff to develop joint solutions to the problems which managers have identified.

Under the legalistic reforms of the past, a bureaucratized organizational structure was created to carry out command-and-control tasks. Inspectors controlled industry and managers controlled inspectors. The end result was a system so inflexible that it was incapable of responding to obvious irrationality in the system. Changing the structure of the organizational environment of regulatory agencies might well bring about corollary changes in the ways that agencies interact with regulated firms.

This reform also faces obstacles, however. In times of fiscal constraints, upgrading the training and professionalism of staff is likely to be viewed as a frill expense. Second, industry may oppose such changes. Industry is likely to argue that lower-level employees should not be given so much authority. Behind this preference for hierarchy, however, may lie industry's interest in being able to influence regulatory action by influencing upper-level managers. De-bureaucratization would decrease industry leverage by eliminating the fulcrum. This would be most true, of course, for those agencies which are captured to some degree. In relation to agencies which currently pursue more legalistic policies, industry may readily recognize the advantages of dealing with a less bureaucratized and more flexible regulatory agency.

Conclusion

Of course, all of these reform proposals have drawbacks as well as advantages. We should not expect to perfect the regulatory system. Although we may attempt to solve the problems of regulation and regulatory bureaucracies by applying the methods of rational-legal and economic analysis, we also need to recognize that regulation exists because there is conflict. Regulation, if it is to be effective, will always hurt some people in order to make other people's lives better. While philosophical principles can help us to sort out what should be done, we may not always have the power to make it so.

Regulation and regulatory reform pose challenging dilemmas which revolve around issues of humanitarianism, fairness, and justice. Regulation forces us to make trade-offs. In addition, as pervasive as regulation is, it is still only one small part of the social world. Regulatory goals must compete with other goals, from health care to national defense, which vie for public attention and resources.

While these factors may place real constraints on the ability of the regulatory system to promote safety, health, honesty, and economic efficiency, awareness of constraints should not paralyze us. Much can be accomplished with the resources already available. It is possible to improve the regulatory system and to devise new ways of mediating the conflicts which give rise to the need for regulation. It is our hope that this survey of the regulatory system will generate discussion leading to new ideas for controlling corporate illegality.

References

Braithwaite, John (1982) "Enforced Self-Regulation: A New Stratgey for Corporate Crime Control." *Michigan Law Review* 80: 1466-1507.

_____(1985) *To Punish or Persuade: Enforcement of Coal Mine Safety*. Albany, NY: State University of New York Press.

Brown, Michael K. (1981) *Working the Street: Police Discretion and the Dilemmas of Reform*. New York: Russell Sage.

Clinard, Marshall B. (1983) *Corporate Ethics and Crime*. Beverly Hills: Sage Publications.

Coffee, John C., Jr. (1981) "'No Soul to Damn; No Body to Kick:' An Unscandalized Inquiry into the Problem of Corporate Punishment." *Michigan Law Review* 79: 386-459.

Fisse, Brent (1985) "Sanctions Against Corporations: The Limitations of Fines and the Enterprise of Creating Alternatives." In Brent Fisse and Peter A. French (eds.) *Corrigible Corporations and Unruly Law*. San Antonio: Trinity University Press.

Fisse, Brent and John Braithwaite (1983) *The Impact of Publicity on Corporate Offenders*. Albany, NY: State University of New York Press.

Fisse, Brent and Peter A. French (1985) *Corrigible Corporations and Unruly Law*. San Antonio: Trinity University Press.

Frank, Nancy (1984) "Policing Corporate Crime: A Typology of Enforcement Styles." *Justice Quarterly* 1: 235-251.

_____(1985) *Crimes Against Health and Safety*. Albany, NY: Harrow and Heston.

Geis, Gilbert (1972) "Criminal Penalties for Corporate Criminals." *Criminal Law Bulletin* (June): 377-392.

Heffron, Florence with Neil McFeeley (1983) *The Administrative Regulatory Process*. New York: Longman.

Lipsky, Michael (1980) *Street-Level Bureaucracy: Dilemmas of the Individual in Public Service*. New York: Russell Sage.

Litan, Robert E. and William D. Nordhaus (1983) *Reforming Federal Regulation*. New Haven: Yale University Press.

Miles, Robert H. and Arvind Bhambri (1983) *The Regulatory Executives*. Beverly Hills: Sage Publications.

Nader, Ralph (1980) "Can a Regulatory Budget Be Calculated?" In Timothy B. Clark, Marvin H. Kosters, and James C. Miller, III (eds.) *Reforming Regulation*. Washington, D.C.: American Enterprise Institute for Public Policy Research.

Perrow, Charles (1970) *Organizational Analysis: A Sociological View*. Monterey, CA: Brooks/Cole.

Rees, Joseph (1986) "Flexible Regulatory Enforcement: A Case Study." Paper presented at the Law and Society Association Annual Meeting, Chicago, Illinois.

Schwartz, Richard D. (1984) "Public Participation in Environmental Protection Proceedings." Working Paper. Syracuse, NY: Syracuse University.

Stone, Christopher D. (1985) "Corporate Regulation: The Place of Social Responsibility." In Brent Fisse and Peter A. French (eds.) *Corrigible Corporations and Unruly Law*. San Antonio: Trinity University Press.

INDEX

Adjudication 5, 25, 79
Administration 24
Administrative law 29, 31, 113
Administrative Procedures Act 31, 32, 45, 79-80, 131-132
Agency capture 73, 89-90, 95, 97, 101-118
    consequences of 111-113
    definitions of 101-103
    incentives toward 104
    prevention of 102, 113-117
    processes of 103-111
    socialization process 106
Aldrin/dieldrin 38-39
American Telephone and Telegraph 64-65
"Amoral calculator" 77-78
Anderson, James E. 101, 118
Antitrust law 2, 13, 20, 50-52, 64, 83-84
Appointment of regulatory officials 104
Ashford, Nicholas A. 50, 74
Auchter, Thorne 58, 104

Baer, Michael A. 106, 120
Bardach, Eugene 11, 25, 43, 46, 51, 54, 55, 70, 72, 74, 77, 85, 87,
                88, 91, 93, 94, 95, 98, 113, 118
Bartrip, Peter W.J. 103, 119
Behrman, Bradley 14, 25, 36, 37, 46
Bernstein, Marver 16, 26, 104, 106, 108, 119
Bhambri, Arvind 33, 39, 46, 108, 132, 137
Braithwaite, John 124, 127, 128, 129, 135, 136
Breyer, Stephen 16, 26, 36, 46
Brown, Michael H. 45, 46
Brown, Michael K. 134, 136

California Occupational Safety and Health Administration 130
Camara v. Municipal Court 67-70, 74
Carcinogens 38-39, 45, 115
Cary, William L. 104, 119